GW00393932

VISITOR'S GUIDE
SUSSEX

Visitor's Guide Series

This series of guide books gives, in each volume, the details and facts needed to make the most of a holiday in one of the tourist areas of Britain and Europe. Not only does the text describe the countryside, villages, and towns of each region, but there is also valuable information on where to go and what there is to see. Each book includes, where appropriate, stately homes, gardens and museums to visit, nature trails, archaeological sites, sporting events, steam railways, cycling, walking, sailing, fishing, country parks, useful addresses — everything to make your visit more worthwhile.

Other titles already published or planned include:
The Lake District (revised edition)
The Chilterns
The Cotswolds
North Wales
The Yorkshire Dales
Cornwall
Devon
East Anglia
Somerset and Dorset
Guernsey, Alderney and Sark
The Scottish Borders
  and Edinburgh
The Welsh Borders
Historic Places of Wales
The North York Moors, York and
  the Yorkshire Coast
Peak District (revised edition)
South and West Wales
Hampshire and the Isle of Wight
Kent
Dordogne (France)
Brittany (France)
Black Forest (W Germany)
The South of France
Tyrol
Loire
French Coast
Iceland

KEY FOR MAPS

	Towns/Villages
═══	Motorways
▬	Mainroads
∿	Rivers
⬯	Lakes/Reservoirs
⊹⊹⊹	Railways
ฅ	Museum/Art Gallery/Centre
π	Archaeological Site
Ħ	Castle/Fort
▲	Ecclesiastical Building
⌂	Building/Country Park
⌒	Cave
❂	Zoo
✳	Other Place of Interest
⌱	Picnic Site

The Visitor's Guide To
SUSSEX

Jim Cleland

MOORLAND PUBLISHING

British Library Cataloguing in
Publication Data

Cleland, J.
    The visitor's guide to Sussex.
    1. Sussex — Description and travel
    — Guide-books
    I. Title
    914.22'504858   DA670.S98

Black and white illustrations were supplied
by:
Arun Tourist Office 15, 95, 98, 99; British
Tourist Authority 35, 40, 63, 66, 67, 69, 73,
76, 81, 90, 92, 100, 112, 116, 118, 124, 126,
128; W.R. Brown 10, 13, 49, 52, 55, 56, 59, 62,
64, 72, 74, 76, 77, 78, 79, 84, 102, 103, 105,
109, 110, 114, 115, 123, 125; Jim Cleland 93,
127; Eastbourne Borough Council 57; East
Sussex County Council 14, 22, 34, 39, 47, 71,
82; Roy Handover 7, 12, 21, 25, 26, 31, 32, 46,
48, 49, 50, 53, 57, 111, 117, 123; G. Ivan
Barnett 20; The National Trust 28-9, 51, 80;
R. Scholes 33, 45.
Colour illustrations were supplied by:
Arun Tourist Board (Arundel Castle and
Arundel); Brighton Borough Council
(Brighton Seafront); Hastings Borough
Council (All Saints Street, Hastings); A.C.G.
Mason (Stopham Bridge, Bosham; Pool
Bridge, Hartfield; Sompting Church;
Michelham Priory); J.A. Robey (Rye);
R.Scholes (Bodiam Castle; Pevensey); South
East England Tourist Board (Alfriston;
Sheffield Park Gardens; Sackville College).

ISBN 0 86190 139 8
ISBN 0 86190 138 X (paperback)

Printed in the UK by
Butler and Tanner Ltd,
Frome, Somerset.
Published by
Moorland Publishing Co Ltd,
Station Street,
Ashbourne, Derbyshire,
DE6 1DE England.
Tel: (0335) 44486

Contents

	Preface	6
	Introduction	7
1	From Rye to Pevensey	18
2	From Pevensey to Lewes	43
3	From Lewes to Brighton and Hove	61
4	Inland Sussex (East)	74
5	From Shoreham to Arundel	88
6	Around Arundel	95
7	From Chichester to the Hampshire Border	105
8	Inland Sussex (West)	120
	Further Information	130
	Bibliography	151
	Index	152

Preface

As a professional blue-badged guide for the South-East there are several recommendations I would like to make to improve your visit to the beautiful county of Sussex.

For instance, the diligent use of tourist information centres and local newspapers is suggested, to discover those local events which no guidebook can adequately cover, but which are the essence of life in Britain.

However, the finest piece of advice I can offer is the professional guide's number one rule: check everything. While every precaution has been taken to ensure that this publication is accurate in every detail, unforeseen changes can occur. For instance, in the South-East over the last few years, one garden has had to close for an additional day because of the wear and tear of feet; another attraction went bankrupt; several National Trust properties have altered their closing days, and a wildlife park has been compulsorily closed. Theatre programmes can change, your chosen attraction may be closed for a special function, or even just through staff shortage due to illness. Therefore, use the telephone numbers which have been included in the Further Information to save yourself a wasted journey, wasted money, and disappointment, particularly when children are involved.

Introduction

Sussex is a maritime county which for administrative purposes has been divided into West Sussex and East Sussex, the county towns being Chichester and Lewes respectively. The county has an area of 1,457 square miles, and the population is approximately $1\frac{1}{4}$ million.

Geology
Except where the English Channel cuts off its eastern end, the Weald is ringed by the chalk Downs. The outward shape of the South Downs is gentle, and is known as a back or dip-shape, but the inward facing slope, or scarp, is very steep.

Within the ring formed by the North and South Downs is another ring of hills formed of the Lower Greensand, separated from the Downs by a narrow vale of Gault Clay. Like the Downs, the sandstone hills have a gentle back-slope and a steep scarp that faces inward towards the centre of the Weald; this sandstone ring has been called the Sandstone Escarpment.

This escarpment overlooks a broad lowland of Weald Clay, the Low Weald, from the middle of which rises the central sandstone core formed by the Hastings Beds. This core is known as the Forest Ridges or High Weald.

At the coast the South Downs break off abruptly at Beachy Head, the High Weald ends in the sandstone cliffs at Hastings, and the Low Weald peters out on the levels at Pevensey and around Rye.

The Hastings Beds which form the core of the Weald are the oldest rocks, deposited possibly 100 million years ago, and they dip underneath the Weald Clay, which in turn is older than the Lower Greensand and dips beneath it.

Within this framework lie variations which have shaped life in Sussex and shaped its history; ironstone in the Weald from Kent to the area around Horsham, alluvial deposits on the coastal plain around Chichester and Worthing, silica sands and gravel in the Weald; now oil has been discovered in both East and West Sussex, and this is being actively prospected throughout the county.

Prehistoric Sussex
The first inhabitants of Sussex date from the early Paleolithic period and their implements have been discovered at Slindon Park and other sites. They lived in the almost sub-tropical conditions before the last Ice Age, and were

Midhurst: one of the earliest Sussex settlements

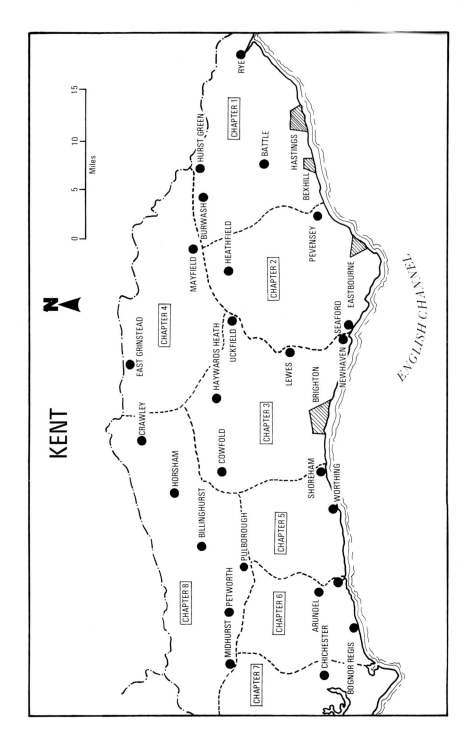

KENT

N

English Channel

Miles
0 5 10 15

RYE
HURST GREEN
CHAPTER 1
BATTLE
HASTINGS
BURWASH
BEXHILL
MAYFIELD
HEATHFIELD
PEVENSEY
CHAPTER 2
EASTBOURNE
EAST GRINSTEAD
CHAPTER 4
SEAFORD
NEWHAVEN
HAYWARDS HEATH
UCKFIELD
LEWES
CRAWLEY
BRIGHTON
COWFOLD
CHAPTER 3
HORSHAM
SHOREHAM
WORTHING
BILLINGHURST
PULBOROUGH
CHAPTER 5
PETWORTH
CHAPTER 8
MIDHURST
CHAPTER 6
ARUNDEL
CHICHESTER
BOGNOR REGIS
CHAPTER 7

probably akin to Neanderthal Man.

The next traces to be found belong to the period when the ice sheets had retreated, some 10,000 years ago. Nomadic hunters crossed what is now the North Sea and were the ancestors of modern man. They made delicately-fashioned flint arrow and spearheads and also carved bone to make fish-hooks and harpoons, examples of all of these having been recovered from sites at Midhurst, Chithurst, and Selmeston near Firle.

Colonisation on a large scale started around 3,000BC by a new wave of settlers, the Neolithic people who originated from the Mediterranean, and who had an advanced social life. Their organisation was such that they were able to undertake enormous projects such as the building of what are known as causewayed camp-forts at Whitehawk and The Trundle, and indeed Avebury and Stonehenge. The long barrow called Bevis's Thumb and the flint mines at Cissbury are also of this period.

Beaker Folk, so-called because of the shape of their drinking vessels, were the next immigrants, ushering in the Bronze Age, although flint implements were still the most commonly used and bronze was scarce and highly prized. These people, probably because of changes in climate, tended to concentrate their settlements within the Weald and avoided the more exposed downland sites. The Beaker Folk, who probably co-existed with the earlier Neolithic settlers, introduced bell or disc barrows for their burials, which can be found throughout Sussex, and settlements have been excavated at Findon and Itford Down.

The Bronze Age, which lasted for well over a thousand years, gradually gave way to the Iron Age, brought by new Celtic settlers who settled in the Weald and began clearing the forests and smelting iron. These new settlers built massive hillforts, sometimes developing previous Neolithic sites, such as those at Cissbury and The Trundle, or establishing massive new fortified hill-cities like Mount Caburn, where excavation in 1932 revealed more than seventy households and a number of crafts and trades. During this period there was also an influx of the Belgae, in the form of a tribe called the Atrebates who colonised the area around Selsey and Chichester under King Cogidubnus, whose palace has been discovered at Fishbourne. He was from the start an ally of Rome.

The Roman Occupation

The conquest of Britain was finally planned under Emperor Claudius in AD42 using the bridgehead established by Cogidubnus, whose unswerving loyalty was mentioned in a letter written by Tacitus to Agricola, the first great Roman Governor of the new province.

In AD43 Claudius with his commander, Aulus Plautius, landed at Richborough in Kent; but in the same year Bosham is known to have been the site of Vespasian's camp, from which he conquered the South-West, which suggests considerable landings of Roman troops in this area. Fishbourne Palace dates in part from approximately this time, and Bosham church almost certainly stands upon the site of a temple dedicated to Mithras, the legion's adopted god.

Sussex, under the *Pax Romanum,* became a prosperous area with a network of major and minor roads; Stane Street being the most widely known. There were many great villas, among them Bignor and Angmering, the fort of *Anderida* or Pevensey, as well as highly developed farming and iron smelting industries.

Between Chichester and Pevensey some twenty villas have been discovered, and their scale and magnificence suggests a social structure and population levels well in excess of most modern estimates. One barn at Bignor measures almost 200ft long, and it is estimated that there were twelve ploughing teams of oxen and over 200

Bosham church stands on the site of an earlier Roman temple

sheep as well as a large number of other beasts.

A section of a Roman road has recently been discovered at Icklesham. It would appear not only that the road from Chichester to Pevensey probably continued to Hythe but also that the Roman road network was greater than hitherto thought. Some idea of production in the iron industry can be gained from the fact that at Beauport Park near Hastings, one slag-heap covered two acres and was over 50ft high, while roads were metalled with iron-slag all over the Weald.

Other important finds are awaiting excavation or decisions regarding their future presentation. One bath house discovered near Hastings is the most complete known, and it is certain that in future years discoveries in Sussex will be contributing greatly to the understanding of this period.

The Saxons

The Roman legions left Britain between AD400 and 410, and the first exact record of Saxon landings occurs in the *Anglo-Saxon Chronicle* for the year 477.

As Roman strength declined and legions were withdrawn to the continent to face Teutonic armies, there were numerous raids which turned into more serious attempts at colonisation. Fishbourne seems to have been a victim of this process, being destroyed in about AD285 and never reoccupied.

The fort of *Anderida* or Pevensey was built around AD250 as part of a chain of fortifications stretching from Hampshire to Kent, and into Suffolk, and although there is now some doubt as to why they were built, they were nevertheless used against the Saxon invaders at a later date, and significantly they became known as the Saxon Shore Forts from the title of the officer commanding the system: 'The Count of the Saxon Shore'.

The *Anglo-Saxon Chronicle* reference for the year AD477 reads: 'This year came Aella to Britain, with his three sons, Cymen, Wlencing, and Cissa, in three ships, landing at a place that is called Cymenshore. There they slew many of the Welsh [Romano-British]; and some in flight they drove into a wood that is called Andredsley.'

In AD490 the Britons made a final stand at Pevensey and were all slain, and it can be said that from that date Sussex belonged to the Saxons. Hastings was colonised by a separate group of Jutish extraction called the Haestingas who maintained a separate existence until AD771 when they were subdued by Offa of Mercia, who conquered Kent and Sussex.

The takeover of Sussex was slow, steady, and complete. Place names became entirely Saxon, and a map of Saxon Sussex differs little from the present day. Towns such as Hastings, Lewes, and Steyning became trading centres, and by AD1000 stone churches such as Worth, Sompting and Bishopstone had been built, influenced by developments across the Channel.

During this period, the ecclesiastical division known as the parish came into being, based upon churches and sub-divided as new churches were built, a system which exists to this day.

Alfred the Great, whose father was buried at Steyning, was forced by pressure from Danish invaders to rebuild the navy, thus acquiring the title of Founder of the English Navy. He probably did this by developing the loose association of ports left behind by the Roman fleet, and therefore could also be said to be the founder of the Cinque Ports fleet.

(It is interesting to note that beneath the throne of Harold as depicted on the Bayeaux Tapestry there are five boats. These have been interpreted as Harold's troubled dreams upon breaking his oath to William, but it is more likely to be a reference to his title of Lord Warden of the Cinque Ports, a position which he assumed along with the throne and which the Normans found significant.)

In 1017 the Witan (Saxon Parliament) chose Canute, a Dane, as king of England and this ended the conflict of the previous two hundred years. Canute regarded England as his home and indeed his daughter was buried in Bosham Church.

Although they had not suffered as much as other parts of the country, the Saxons of Sussex must have been relieved that the Danish threat was removed. There had been numerous raids within the county, and in 895 Chichester was attacked by a Danish army, but the invaders were driven off with heavy losses. The entire coast of Sussex was subjected to further attacks over the next hundred years, and in AD994 and again in AD1000, the *Anglo-Saxon Chronicle* notes 'burning, plundering, and manslaughter' everywhere in Sussex.

The reign of Canute was a prosperous one for Sussex. He died in 1035, and seven years later Edward the Confessor ascended to the throne, so setting in motion the chain of events which led to the most famous battle in English history in 1066.

Edward had in 1001 married Emma, daughter of Richard the Fearless, Duke of Normandy, and started a long association with the Normans, culminating in his promise to William when he visited England in 1051 to allow him to suceed to the English crown. He had already given the manor of Rameslie, which included much of Hastings and the surrounding area, to the Abbey of Fécamp, and this connection may have ultimately determined William's invasion plans.

The Norman Conquest
When in 1066 the Witan chose Harold Godwinsson as king, William sent ambassadors to claim the crown on the basis of the promise made by Edward the Confessor, and of the oath of fealty made by Harold when in Normandy in 1064. These claims were rejected and plans for the Norman invasion were laid.

In September 1066, Harold Hardrada,

King of Norway, and Harold Godwinsson's brother Tostig, landed in the north and Harold Godwinsson marched to meet them at Stamford Bridge. In the ensuing battle both Hardrada and Tostig were slain and the invading army totally defeated.

In the meantime a favourable wind had enabled William to land his army at Pevensey, and Harold was forced to rush south to meet this new threat. The weakened and exhausted Saxon army was defeated after a fierce battle on 14 October, 1066; and by 1071, having crushed a series of revolts, William was the undisputed King of England. There then began a period when Sussex was the most important part of that kingdom.

The county was divided into six divisions, or Rapes, each with a castle, a port, and a river. To rule these divisions William appointed his most trusted followers, who commenced a programme of building unrivalled until Victorian times. Castles, cathedrals, churches, dwellings, and ports were built or developed throughout the county, and in addition abbeys such as at Battle were commenced, and the Domesday survey was started.

The Middle Ages

This period saw the rise to great importance of the Cinque Ports, and for a period in the twelfth century Hastings became head port of the Confederation. Rye and Winchelsea were added to the Confederation as the 'Two Antient Towns' with full Cinque Ports status.

In 1264 at Lewes, Simon de Montfort defeated Henry III and the resulting treaty, the Mise of Lewes, is generally reckoned to mark the beginning of parliamentary government.

The Hundred Years' War led to the Channel ports being subjected to a series of disastrous raids by the French. Rye, Winchelsea, Hastings, Brighton, Rottingdean, Shoreham, and Seaford were all attacked and seriously damaged between 1337 and 1448, while the portsmen inflicted similar havoc along the French coast.

All this naval activity led to a sharp increase in boatbuilding and general port usage. The Confederation of the Cinque Ports and the Brotherhood of Guestling (the Sussex Ports) had a membership of seven head-ports, and thirty-nine incorporated or unincorporated 'limbs' or sub-ports,

Pevensey Castle, part of the Roman 'Saxon Shore' defence, dates from 250

Lewes castle saw several battles and an important treaty

producing a channel fleet of some hundred vessels, as well as cargo vessels, and fishing boats. The oak trees of the Weald were extensively felled to supply shipyards from Rye to Chichester, and the iron industry, relatively neglected by the Saxons, underwent a revival. Timber-beamed houses began to appear, complete with glass windows made in the area around Billingshurst and Horsham.

Castle building had all but ceased due to the advent of the siege gun, and the contrast between the battlements of Bodiam, built between 1385-90 and probably the last functional castle to be built, and the stylised castle at Herstmonceux of 1440, is very sharp. Nevertheless, from the end of the twelfth century to the beginning of the fifteenth century most of the principal Norman castles were enlarged. There was also a surge in the building or extending of churches and manor houses; many of those in Sussex date from this period.

Tudor Sussex

The assumption of the throne by Henry VII coincided with the rise of the Sussex iron industry. Aided by Huguenot refugees who brought new skills and techniques from the continent, blast furnaces mushroomed throughout the Weald and the manufacture of ordnance grew rapidly.

A Royal Commission in 1573 reported well over a hundred furnaces operating in the Wealden forests, and by 1607 serious doubts were being expressed about wisdom of the widespread

Bodiam, probably the last functional castle to be built

destruction of trees. The now delightful villages of Sedlescombe, Robertsbridge, Mayfield, and Frant echoed to the roar of furnaces and the sound of water-driven forge hammers. Sedlescombe and Robertsbridge contained large ordnance factories, and in Buxted the first cast cannon was made; a lively trade in smuggling such weapons to the continent was in existence long before brandy, 'baccy' and lace ever changed hands.

Families rose to great wealth, and many fine Wealden houses were built by the so-called iron masters. Batemans at Burwash, Wakehurst Place, and Sheffield Park are such buildings; and almost all building in Sussex during the reign of the Tudors, and indeed up to the time of George II, was in some way financed by iron.

Another notable feature of East Sussex, which appeared some time during the sixteenth century, was the oast-house; that quaint conical hop-drying oven introduced by the Huguenots. An old rhyme says, 'Turkey, carp, hops, pickerel, and beer, came into England all in one year'. That year was probably round about 1520.

Around 1530, when Henry VIII was having difficulty in persuading the Pope that his divorce was desirable, it was thought prudent to build fresh fortifications along the South Coast. One of these forts, Camber Castle, with the configuration of a Tudor rose, was built between Rye and Winchelsea in 1539.

Another result of the royal disagreement with Rome was the dissolution of the abbeys. Battle Abbey was given to Sir Anthony Browne, Keeper of the King's Horses in 1538. Sir Thomas Cromwell, in his role as Vicar-General, travelled in procession through Sussex in 1539, dissolving Bayham, Wilmington, Michelham, and Boxgrove Abbeys, as well as many lesser establishments in 1539. However, he should perhaps have been more circumspect in exposing himself to heavenly wrath, because he was executed on Tower Hill in 1540, for the treasonable act of advising his king to marry Anne of Cleves.

Sussex did not exert an overt influence over the defeat of the Spanish Armada, as the ports were only able to send a few small ships, but in other very real ways, the county played an important role. The English ships were made of Sussex oak, used cannon cast in Sussex from Sussex iron, using Sussex gunpowder to fire Sussex cannonballs. Their ropes and sails were made in Sussex and they used a device invented by a man called Fletcher from Rye which enabled them to sail against the wind.

The Stuarts and the Commonwealth
After the death of Elizabeth I in 1603, and the renewed bitterness between Protestants and Catholics which led to the Gunpowder Plot in 1605, the people of Sussex began to form alignments which later determined which side they supported in the Civil War.

In Lewes, bitter memories were aroused of the burning of the seventeen martyrs by order of Queen Mary in 1555-7, and to this day the Bonfire Boyes of Lewes carry an effigy of the then Pope, Paul the Fifth, to be burned with cries of 'No Popery'.

East Sussex in general inclined towards Protestantism, and the impetus of the Gunpowder Plot combined with the everyday activities of charcoal burning, faggot making, gunpowder manufacture and boat building, readily made the November bonfire nights which are so justly famous. Only Hastings, which was strongly Royalist, and newcomers like Eastbourne, do not have an organised bonfire night; the calender of celebrations starts in September and carries on until

Arundel Castle was much fought-over in the Civil war

December, involving most towns and villages in East Sussex.

West Sussex, and in particular Chichester, saw much more of the Civil War, changing hands several times; Arundel Castle was pounded nearly flat by General Waller's forces who mounted cannon on a nearby church tower. The Weald was of course supplying weapons for the war, and both sides wanted to control Sussex, both for this reason and for access to the continent, which must have been particularly prized by Prince Charles who escaped via Shoreham after the Battle of Worcester in 1651.

The Wealden forges were now also producing all manner of domestic ware: fire-backs, nails and screws of all sizes, hinges, fire grates, fan-driven spits, and many other products including wrought ironwork and railings, but this was to prove their swan song as, by 1717, due to a shortage of wood and the development of smelting by coke, only twenty furnaces remained in Sussex; the last one, at Ashburnham, was extinguished in 1820.

Sussex was not greatly affected by the Civil War, and suffered little of the damage to churches and religious buildings that took place in other areas.

Georgian Sussex
This architectural period, roughly between 1700 and 1830, saw the beginnings of two very important influences: smuggling, and the seaside resort.

Two major smuggling gangs operated in Sussex, the Alfriston Gang which operated in the area between Eastbourne and Brighton, and the Hawkhurst Gang which operated around Rye. Both of these gangs, which continued to operate throughout the Napoleonic Wars, were using the same methods which had started with the illegal export of wool, rope, and ordnance, and then reversed to bring in tea, perfume, spirits, and lace from the continent.

Very few people remained uninvolved with this trade, and entire towns such as Burwash, burdened with the unemployment of a declining iron industry, were maintained largely by smuggling. Houses were built with hiding places incorporated, and many more than the four and twenty ponies mentioned by Kipling in his poem were kept as transport. Wesley himself could not get them to stop, and the courts could not, or would not, prosecute. In one year it was estimated that the government lost £1 million in duty on tea alone, and in the 1790s two thirds of all tobacco smoked was smuggled. The government clearly could not allow such a state of affairs to continue, and the Coastguard Service and the village policeman were both introduced around 1830 to combat the activities of the smugglers.

Seaside resorts came into being partly as a result of increasing spending power. Dr Russell's advocacy of the theraputic qualities of seawater in 1750 and the Prince of Wales's liaison with Mrs Fitzherbert turned humble Brighthelmstone into fashionable Brighton; the public took to this new fad and the seaside resort was born.

Where Brighton led others followed, and soon Bognor and Worthing, Eastbourne and St Leonards were luring society figures to the 'delights' of being immersed in the sea and even drinking sea water, to cure them of their excesses.

During Georgian times the timbered fronts of Tudor houses were regarded as mean and vulgar. As a result many old houses were re-fronted while retaining their Tudor core and probably every town in Sussex has examples. The same applied to country houses, many of which, Petworth and Uppark for example, were remodelled.

The coaching era followed the advent of the turnpike system in the late seventeenth century. It became possible to travel from London to Brighton in under six hours, and regular services were run from all the major Sussex towns, most of which have retained their old coaching inns.

Capability Brown came to Sussex during this period and he remodelled such parks as Petworth, Goodwood, Arundel, and Sheffield Park with predictably beautiful results. The landscape was further modified by the keeping of sheep on the downs, increased ploughing, orchards, and market gardens, and the appearance of windmills, of which several hundred were built between 1700 and 1820. Until the great reform act of 1832, which caused innumerable riots, Sussex had had a greater share than most counties of 'rotten boroughs' (constituencies with no, or very few voters) and 'pocket boroughs' (constituencies held by the nominees of the landowner). Rye had returned two members as a pocket borough, one of which was the Duke of Wellington, whose government bitterly opposed the 1832 Act. Rye was subsequently reduced to one MP, as were Arundel, Horsham and Midhurst. Bramber; East Grinstead, Seaford, Steyning and Winchelsea were reduced to none at all.

Victoria to the Present

The coming of the railway opened up the county for trade and tourism, and by 1863 all the main lines into Sussex were completed. This was accompanied by a great wave of building and an increase in industry. Brighton railway works came into being, and Hastings, Brighton, Worthing, Eastbourne and other towns began to reach out and engulf the villages and countryside around them; a trend which has continued until now.

In places the Martello towers of Pitt stand close to the concrete pill-boxes of 1940. The occasional row of pyramid-shaped tank traps remind the viewer of times when England faced the might of the Third Reich with pikes and World War I rifles. Sussex was well-nigh evacuated at this time with hordes of labelled mothers and children being taken by train to Wales and the West Country. The coast was closed and the beaches were mined. 'Dad's Army' was not a comedy but a reality and the small, often bullet riddled, boats drawn up on the banks of Sussex harbours were a stark reminder of Dunkirk.

Most of the coastal towns received quite heavy bombing, and later had the doodle-bug to contend with; Rye, in particular, received hostile attention out of all proportion to its size and importance.

After the war, when the bomb sites were cleared and the beaches made safe, people came back to Sussex in force, many of them to stay. The village of Crawley was designated a New Town, and expansion started in 1947. The population of Sussex has grown steadily, so far without irreparable damage, but the danger signals are there, and many people, residents and visitors alike, are striving to keep it as one of the finest counties in England.

1 From Rye to Pevensey

The Norman division of Sussex was the Rape, of which there were six, Hastings Rape being the most easterly. Each Rape contained a castle, and a port, and each was assigned to a totally trusted supporter; in this case Robert, Count of Eu. It was Robert who, between 1068 and 1080, built the castle which still watches Hastings today, to replace the prefabricated timber fort which was hastily erected when William first landed; the timber fort at Hastings was his first construction on English soil.

Hastings, however, existed long before the battle to which it gave its name was fought. There is evidence of Iron Age hillforts at Hastings on East Cliff and Castle Hill. The people who occupied them were of the Belgae tribe, related to the Atrebates who occupied Gaul and the Chichester region; Julius Caesar said that these people supplied reinforcements to his Gallic enemies and this was one of the reasons for his foray in 55BC. The Belgae were able sailors using sailing vessels rather than galleys, which sailed to many parts of the continent from a harbour which occupied the area where the Priory cricket ground stands today.

Again, there is evidence of a Roman camp and channel fleet port at Hastings; the Saxon and Jute settlers always referred to Hastings as *Haestenchester*, the chester being from *castra*, a camp, which indicates a Roman base. As it is unlikely that the Romans would have left a gap in their 'Saxon Shore' defences from Lympne to Pevensey, and as all the other members of the original Confederation of Cinque Ports were Roman centres, then the case becomes strong. And if finally the fact that the representatives of the Cinque Ports who carry the canopy at coronations are called Barons, as are the free men, is, as the historian Coke maintains, 'indupidable proof of the Roman origin of the corporate body in which it is used', then there can be little doubt that Hastings is one of the missing links in the Roman Saxon Shore chain of defences.

Hastings derives its name from Haesten, chief of the Haestingas, a mixed group of Saxons, Jutes, and some Danes who occupied this area in a separate kingdom until defeated by King Offa in AD771 when it was annexed into the kingdom of Mercia. The town became so important that in AD924 King Athelstan established a mint, and coins were minted here in the reigns of Canute, Edward the Confessor, Harold, William I, William II, and Henry I. Silver pennies discovered at Alfriston in 1843 included one rare coin of Hardicanute.

By the time of Edward the Confessor, the Cinque Ports were formally incorporated under the government of a Lord Warden, an appointment directly descended from the Roman Count of the Saxon Shore, the later Saxon Guardian of the Ports, extending in an unbroken chain of office up to Queen Elizabeth the Queen Mother who currently holds the position.

At the time of William the Conqueror's landing at Pevensey, and his subsequent march to secure Hastings, it is reported that the town, influenced no doubt by the fact that it belonged partially to the Abbey of Fécamp, opened its gates to William and offered only limited resistance. The scene of a blazing house on the Bayeaux Tapestry shows what happened to those who resisted.

Within four years of his accession,

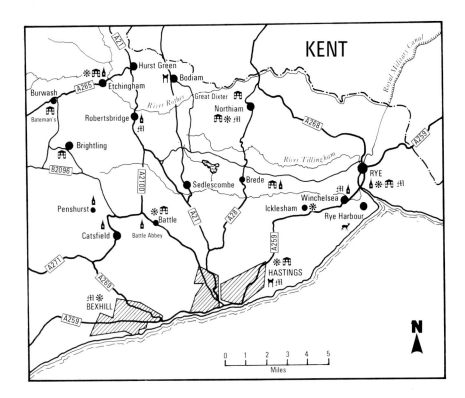

William had established his
administrative centre at Hastings and
had reconfirmed the status of the Cinque
Ports. Work had commenced on the
Domesday survey in which Hastings
appears under the title of New Burgh.
The New Burgh referred to was the area
now known as the Old Town, which was
then being established in the Bourne
valley. This move was due to silting of
the old harbour, and erosion by the sea
of the cliffs at White Rock and Castle
Hill where the previous town was sited.

In the next hundred years Hastings
reached the zenith of its importance,
with charters granted in 1149 and 1155.
Subsequently, great storms in the
thirteenth century, notably in 1250 and
1287, signalled the end of its port by
destroying the harbour. A further blow
to the status of Hastings was the loss of
Normandy in 1204 which removed a
great deal of the cross channel trade.

This led to the dismantling of the castle
in 1216 by King John, who feared that it
might be taken and used by French
invaders.

The Hundred Years' War, which
began in 1337, was the start of a period
when the coastal towns of Kent and
Sussex were subjected to murderous
assaults by the French; they were
frequently destroyed, with great loss of
life. Hastings was attacked in 1339, and
again in 1360, 1378 and 1380.

By 1294, Hastings was only able to
furnish three ships despite having the
additional support of 'limbs' at Seaford,
Pevensey, Northeye, Bulverhythe,
Hydneye, and Bekesbourne, and by the
start of the fifteenth century the original
town was completely abandoned. The
priory, which stood where the cricket
ground now stands, was abandoned
after inundation; Sir John Pelham
offered the monks land at Warbleton in

19

View of Hastings from the castle

1413, and by 1440 the valley was a swamp.

What is now the Old Town did not escape in the French raids and both St Clements Church and All Saints are built on the sites of earlier churches ruined during the raids of 1378 and 1380. The rebuilding of St Clements was commenced in about 1381, that of All Saints not until 1436.

After all these catastrophic events Hastings ceased to be of major significance as a port, although ceaseless efforts have been made to revive the harbour; efforts which are still continuing. Oddly enough, in spite of the handicap of having to draw vessel straight up on to the shingle of the foreshore, one of the principal trades during the sixteenth and seventeenth centuries was boat building. This continued in some measure until the last century; the lugger *Enterprise*, now in

the Fisherman's Museum, was the last boat to be built, and was completed in 1909.

Throughout the eighteenth century smuggling was rife in the area, the poor harbourage assisting rather than hindering 'Ruxley's Crew' as the Hastings gang was known. Landings took place at Galley Hill near Bexhill, Bulverhythe, and at various inlets along the cliffs at Fairlight and Ecclesbourne. Boat building and smuggling were combined to mutual benefit. One vessel, *The Plough*, had a false bow which concealed fifty kegs.

Towards the end of the eighteenth century the first patients began to arrive to take the air and bathe. During the first thirty years of the nineteenth century Hastings expanded and began once again to occupy the area abandoned four hundred years earlier. Wellington Square was constructed in

20

Unique net stands on the Stade

1824, the first stone of St Leonards was laid in 1828 and by 1855 Warrior Square was almost completed. The Pier arrived in 1872, originally accompanied by another opposite the Royal Victoria Hotel built in 1891, but this did not survive World War II and was dismantled.

The inter-war years brought the Bathing Pool, now a holiday camp at the western end of St Leonards, Bottle Alley which runs from the pier to Warrior Square, the White Rock Pavilion, and what are believed to be Britain's first underground car-parks, still in use.

However, despite all the changes over the years the Old Town remains the jewel in Hastings' crown. The beach at the east end of the town immediately below where High Street and All Saints Street climb the hill, is called The Stade, a Saxon word meaning landing place. This name is singularly appropriate as boats are still winched up on to the shingle straight from the sea to lie like a seal colony along the beach.

The Stade is famous for the net sheds which stand by the short road to Rock-a-Nore. These tall timber structures were introduced in Tudor times and are used for storing tackle and nets. They are unique in Britain and are believed to owe their configuration to a desire to occupy a small ground space and so avoid taxes. A little further along the Rock-a-Nore road lies the Fisherman's Museum in a chapel dating from 1854, and above it all towers the East Hill lift which climbs the cliff to Hastings Country Park, unless of course a climb from Tackleway up 227 steps is more to your taste.

All Saints Street and High Street run parallel northwards from The Stade, a picturesque jumble of architectural styles blending in the way that many buildings did before the nineteenth century. At the bottom of All Saints Street is the site of a former landing stage now occupied by a quaint old building called Pulpit Gate, and further up is an even more quaint triangular house called the Piece of Cheese. Many stories have been told to explain the unusual shape; wagers nearly always figure in them, but the sad truth is that the Piece of Cheese derives its shape entirely from a commercial desire to create a saleable house on a very limited plot.

Near the top of All Saints Street lies Shovells, reputedly the oldest house in the Old Town. It belonged to the mother of Admiral Sir Cloudesley Shovell, and a touching story is told that once, when sailing past Hastings, he came ashore to crave her blessing and press ten guineas into her aged hand, after which he left with a tear in his eye: understandable, as the gift is worth £1,000 by modern standards.

Nearly opposite Shovells is an old pub called The Stag which has on display two mummified cats which were discovered during alterations. As this phenomenon has been observed in other Old Town houses it could be concluded that witchcraft was being practised in that area, and that this represented some form of protection against evil, or perhaps harm from the sea.

At the top of All Saints Street stands the church which gives it the name. Perpendicular in style, it dates from early in the fifteenth century, and has an interesting 'Doom' painting over the

All Saints' Street, Hastings

chancel arch, and a curious brass to Thomas Goodenough and his wife. The notorious Titus Oates of 'Popish Plot' fame was a curate here, while on a pleasanter note, the graveyard contains the tomb of one George Mogridge, who under the name of Old Humphrey wrote childrens stories. The avenue nearby was named after him, and at one time had Wellington's house at the top.

The junction of All Saints Street and The Bourne marks the spot where the old market cross used to stand. It is now graced, by the beautiful Stables Theatre which presents high quality talks, art, plays, and other activities, showing what dedication and flair can do.

The Bourne contains little of interest

East Hill Lift
Cliff railway leading to Hastings Country Park. Panoramic view of the harbour.

Hastings Castle
Remains of William the Conqueror's first castle with whispering gallery and dungeon. Built between 1068 and 1080 by Robert, Count of Eu, Lord of Hastings Rape.

Hastings Country Park
520 acres of cliffwalks and glens with tremendous views.

Hastings Embroidery, Town Hall
Twenty-seven panels depicting English history 1066-1966, especially commissioned from the Royal College of Needlework.

Hastings Model Village, White Rock
Miniature Tudor village amid splendid gardens.

St Clements Caves
Nearly three acres of smugglers' caves and tunnels.

The Stade
Picturesque fishing quarter with unique net-sheds.

Fisherman's Museum, Rock-A-Nore
The history of fishing and the fishermen of Hastings. Also the lugger *Enterprise*.

Hastings Museum, Cambridge Road
Local ethnology, zoology, and geology, plus wealden iron and Sussex pottery. The Durbar Room contains collections from Asia and Oceania.

until one is almost back at The Stade. There a nondescript chapel hides the fact that it was once a theatre where the legendary Grimaldi performed.

Opposite, the unusually named Winding Street has a small section of the town wall through which the sea and the French both burst with disastrous results. The Bourne gets its name from the river which ran down the valley, and Winding Street from the winding or blowing of the moot horn at midnight when a mayor was to be elected. And heaven help him if he refused to serve after such honour was conferred upon him, for Hastings, in common with the other Cinque Ports, had a law that such refusal rendered the ingrate liable to have his house beaten down!

The building where the High Street joins The Bourne, Old Hastings House, was once the residence of the poet Coventry Patmore. He was responsible for the building of the church which stands next to The Stables Theatre in 1884, and he contributed to the cost. This Roman Catholic Church, St Mary Star-Of-The-Sea, contains a chantry which is a memorial to his wife.

High Street runs back down to The Stade and is a rare mixture of architectural styles and antique shops, with a raised pavement on one side. Looking at it now it is hard to realise that it quite recently carried two-way traffic, including buses and trolley-buses. The numerous alleys which duck between the houses in the Old Town, which would be called ginnels in the north, are called twittens here. There is one which runs from Winding Street to High Street and emerges nearly opposite the oldest church in Hastings, St Clements.

St Clements, which lies just off the High Street, was built on the site of an earlier church destroyed by the French in 1378. Perpendicular in style, it was commenced around 1380. The stone cannon balls on the tower have rather different histories. One was found embedded in the tower after passing French and Dutch warships fired on the town in 1720; the other, it is said, was added purely for reaons of symmetry!

Dante Gabriel Rossetti married Elizabeth Siddal here in 1860. Rossetti, with Millais and Holman Hunt, was a founder of the Pre-Raphaelite school of painting.

The flight of steps near St Clements leads up to the castle and the caves. It is also possible to take a lift from George Street. St Clements Caves have an area of some three acres and are reputed to have been used by smugglers in the eighteenth century, although they were considerably extended in the nineteenth century.

Hastings Castle was built by Robert, Count of Eu between 1068 and 1080, together with a church which numbered Thomas à Becket and William of Wykeham, founder of Winchester College and New College, Oxford, as Dean and Prebendary respectively. In 1201 King John promulgated from here his declaration of English supremacy over the seas; as he was fighting a losing battle to keep Normandy, the declaration had a somewhat hollow ring. By 1204 Normandy was lost, and the vaunted supremacy was such that in 1216 King John returned to slight the castle to prevent it being taken and used by the French. It was restored by Henry III, but constant erosion by the sea destroyed the cliff upon which it stands so that by the sixteenth century only part of the castle, and that in ruins, remained standing. The West Hill is one of the best vantage points from which to overlook The Stade and the Old Town.

The opposite hill, the East Hill, is at one end of Hastings Country Park which runs across the cliffs some five miles to Cliff End at Pett. This area has long been acknowledged as one of the most beautiful on the south coast, containing heathland, woods, tumbling streams, and what old guides used to describe as 'verdant pasturelands'. There are several notable spots within the park: Fairlight Glen, Ecclesbourne Glen, the Fire Hills (which get their name from the blaze of gorse flowers), and Lovers' Seat or Leap.

Lovers' Leap is supposedly where a Miss Boys from nearby Fairlight Hall used to signal to her lover, Captain Lamb from Rye, as his ship patrolled the coast. Legend has it that when Miss Boys was refused permission to marry the socially inferior captain, she became crazed with grief and threw herself to her death from this spot. The less dramatic, but much more pleasant truth, however, is that the couple eloped to London and were married at St Clement Danes, and lived happily ever after.

An iguanadon's footprint was found at this spot as a result of the constant erosion along this stretch of coast. Visitors are warned, literally on peril of their lives, not to venture too close to the cliff edges which are often under-cut and ready to fall.

Fairlight church represents the highest point in this area (599ft) and nearby there is an interpretation centre, where leaflets of the various trails can be obtained. They are also available at the two tourist centres in Hastings. Fairlight Church is a nondescript Victorian building where probably the only interesting feature is the grave of Richard D'Oyley Carte.

Back in Hastings, moving west along the sea-front, Pelham Crescent, very reminiscent of Nash's terraces in Brighton, is rather pleasant, and was recessed into the cliff below the castle in 1828. The sea-front forms part of the A259 coast road which leads to Bexhill and Eastbourne, past the pier built in 1872, and the White Rock Pavilion which presents summer programmes of top variety acts and winter programmes of classical music played by leading symphony orchestras.

About the stretch between St Leonards and Bexhill it is impossible to be polite or silent. It is ugly, dreary, and incapable of coping with the volume of traffic which uses it, particularly during the morning and evening; a tasteless example of 1930s ribbon development. It was on the shore here that the *Amsterdam*, flagship of the Dutch East

Part of the De La Warr pavilion, Bexhill

India Company was wrecked. Dutch experts are eventually hoping to raise the ship and return it to Holland. Some of the artefacts from this wreck can be seen at Hastings Museum.

Bulverhythe, a little further towards Bexhill, is the site of a lost port. William is supposed to have landed here while taking Hastings, falling flat on his face, to the dismay of his superstitious followers. With the quick wits which were to save the Normans during the famous battle, he quieted their fears and restored his dignity by rising with a handful of sand and crying 'I have taken siezin of England'. Nothing remains at Bulverhythe except the remains of the ancient chapel of St Mary behind the Bull Inn, which was a notorious haunt of smugglers and convenient to their landing place.

Bexhill is often dismissed as dull, genteel, and part of the 'Costa Geriatrica'. Yet Bexhill offers some of the best and friendliest shopping in the area. It is clean, decent, has good beaches, and generally represents values long departed in many towns that claim superiority. For those who do not want discos or high-technology entertainment, Bexhill offers a pleasant family holiday and an excellent touring centre.

Bexelei is mentioned in the Domesday Book and the parish church contains Saxon work. The manor was a residence of the Bishops of Chichester until the Dissolution. It now contains a costume museum, and open-air theatre is performed in the grounds. The main theatre is of course the De La Warr Pavilion built to the design of Erich Mendelsohn and Serge Chermayoff in 1933-6. The De La Warr offers a wide range of entertainment including sporting events.

From Bexhill to Battle the road passes through Catsfield and Ninfield.

Colonnade on the Esplanade, St Leonards

Catsfield Church, St Lawrence, dates in
part from the beginning of the twelfth
century, while nearby Catsfield Place is
sixteenth century. Marie Antoinette sent
her jewels to Catsfield Place, which
possesses a staircase originally belonging
to Hampton Court Palace, and one of
those mythical tunnels which supposedly
travel for miles throughtout England.
This one is reputed to reach Battle
Abbey, some two miles away!

The village of Crowhurst was, with
the other villages in the area, laid waste
by William to draw Harold to the coast.
Harold in fact owned the manor, and the
yew tree in the churchyard was probably
well established in 1066. It is interesting
that the only yew tree of comparable age
is also next to a St George's church and
also at another Crowhurst, in Surrey.
The ruins to the south of the church are
the remains of the thirteenth-century
manor house which once belonged to
John, Earl of Richmond.

Ninfield has recently won a best-kept-
village award for Sussex and is indeed a

kempt little place. Its stocks and whipping post are still in position near the church, possibly waiting for a fresh lease of life curbing those who drop litter.

The road from Catsfield finally reaches a junction with the A269 near Ashburnham where the last Sussex iron furnace was extinguished in 1820, having spent the latter part of its existence making the cast iron firebacks so typical of the Weald. Ashburnham Place, now a religious centre, was the seat of the Earls of Ashburnham, and contains relics of Charles I. There is an area near here with the intriguing name of Brownbread Street, possibly derived from the similarity of the lumps of iron slag on the Roman road to brown loaves.

Penhurst and Dallington are also in this area of woods and coppices, which even today still gives the feeling of being remote. The church at Penhurst is recommended as a good example of Decorated and Perpendicular church architecture. Dallington has the Sugar Loaf, a peculiar conical folly said to have been built to win a bet by a local eccentric, Squire John (Mad Jack Fuller). He also built the nearby Brightling Observatory and is buried under a massive pyramid in Brightling churchyard. It is said that Fuller bet that he could see the spire of Dallington church from his home, and upon finding that he could not, had this edifice hurriedly erected. He also built an obelisk called Brightling Needle and saved Bodiam Castle from ruin.

Fuller was a colourful character. Weighing in at around twenty stone, he travelled to the House of Commons as MP for East Sussex in a vast coach built like a farm cart, which was heavily armed and stuffed with provisions. As an additional precaution he had armed outriders. He was once imprisoned in the Tower for calling the Speaker an 'insignificant little man in a wig', and the fortune he inherited came from iron and slavery, which he supported. It is also possible that Mad Jack supplemented his income by organising smuggling in the area, and cultivated eccentricity was a useful cover. The evidence is all circumstantial but nonetheless convincing.

The wall around his home, Rose Hill (now called Brightling Park) was ostensibly built to help the unemployed, but also effectively hid what was happening inside. The Observatory was built as a result of his interest in astronomy, but also commanded a view of a huge stretch of the coast and was ideally placed to be a signalling station. The follies, for which there are either weak explanations or none, were hollow and placed on known smugglers' routes where the coast runners handed goods over to the inland smugglers to transport to London. Nearby Burwash specialised in such trade, and the follies were ideally placed dropping points from which the Burwash men could collect.

Even the saving of Bodiam Castle could be suspect. In Fuller's day the Rother was navigable to that point, and a search of boats laden with stone, ordered by an eccentric for saving a useless castle would be unlikely. However, Bodiam was well placed for the Burwash pack-men, and convenient to the roads to Maidstone and Tonbridge.

Finally, it must be remembered that smuggling started as an export trade, one of the principal items of which was ordnance, which the Fuller family manufactured. When smuggling became an import trade, the shipping arrangements were simply used in reverse, and as many of the ironmasters and their men had initiated the trade, they simply remained involved in smuggling of goods into England. As a final point, why was he always so heavily guarded?

Burwash was, as already stated, an inland smuggling town with practically every household involved. This was not unusual, for as the iron industry declined and unemployment grew, most of the Wealden towns got caught up in the new 'industry'. It is a charming village with many beautiful houses along its main street, which is also noted for pollarded lime trees along one side. Burwash, will now however always be known as the home of Rudyard Kipling.

Batemans, a National Trust property, was Kipling's home from 1902 until his death in 1936, and his study has been preserved just as he left it. The house was reputedly built by a local ironmaster, one John Brittan, in 1634 from stone quarried locally. Kipling fell in love with it at once, designing the gardens and installing a unique turbine in the watermill to generate electricity.

Etchingham is the village next to Burwash. Not as picturesque perhaps, but with a very notable church and a very interesting new enterprise. The church of St Mary and St Nicholas is considered to be the finest fourteenth-century church in Sussex, being almost exactly as it was when built by Sir William de Etchingham in 1363. There are several Etchingham brasses including one of 1388 commemorating Sir William himself, and there is a rather fine weather-vane bearing the de Etchingham arms.

The enterprise is at nearby Haremere Hall, a dignified seventeenth-century manor house, Lady Killearn, the owner, and John and Brenda Lavis have introduced working heavy horses in a shire horse centre. This is not a side-show to entertain day trippers, but a hard-headed business enterprise to integrate these gentle giants into all aspects of the working of the estate, and to determine their viability in modern farming conditions. There is also a breeding programme to reproduce the carthorse of pre-war days. The horses — Shires, Ardennes, a Suffolk Punch, Welsh cobs and others — are presented twice a day. There is also a nature trail, an adventure playground, picnic sites, cart rides, and furthermore the food is home-made and appetising.

Robertsbridge lies back down the A21 towards Battle. There is more to it than

Bateman's

meets the eye, for away from the constant traffic there are quiet places with Tudor houses. In 1176 Robert de St Martin founded the Cistercian Abbey which now forms part of Abbey Farm. He probably built the bridge soon after for in 1200 Robertsbridge started being referred to as de Ponte Roberti.

Salehurst forms the other part of this parish, and the parish church is there. It dates from the early part of the

thirteenth century, being one of those churches built for the workers of the abbey; Battle church had similar beginnings.

Robertsbridge is also known as the home of the cricket bat. The firm of Grey-Nicholls, which grew from the hobby of L. J. Nicholls in the 1870s, has furnished bats for many of the world's great players, starting with W. G Grace. Interestingly, Horace Walpole on a journey through Sussex found all accommodation in Robertsbridge occupied by smugglers. Further on, he

found another inn but this one was 'crammed with excise officers'.

The A21 is notorious locally, being known as the 'snail trail' due to its many twists and turns. The A2100 spur which leaves the A21 at Johns Cross leads to Battle in a more direct way; probably a minor Roman iron road.

Battle owes its existence to the Battle of Senlac Hill, erroneously called the Battle of Hastings. The town grew around the abbey dedicated to St Martin, which William had vowed to build if he were successful against the

The Abbey of St Martin, Battle (DoE)
Built to fulfil a vow made by the Conqueror before the fateful battle of 1066 and standing upon the actual battlefield, the abbey was consecrated by St Anselm in 1094. The dorter and refectory of William's abbey, the battlefield, and the great gatehouse of 1338 are still standing on Senlac Hill.

Pilgrims Rest, Battle
Former almonry of the abbey; a timber-framed wealden hall-house built in 1420 and once a hospice for pilgrims.

Battle Museum
Local history and the events of 1066 including a diorama and Bayeaux Tapestry reproduction in prints.

Bodiam Castle, Bodiam (NT)
Castle of 1385-90, set in a water-lilied moat, built to withstand French raids.

Batemans, Burwash (NT)
Home of Rudyard Kipling from 1902 to 1936, and kept as he left it. Built in 1634 with beautiful grounds and a working watermill.

Haremere Hall, Etchingham
Home of the Sussex shire horses with working heavy horses in the grounds of a seventeenth-century manor house.

St Georges Vineyard, Heathfield
Five acres offering tours, tasting, and food, as well as sales of wine.

Gray-Nicholls, Robertsbridge
Tours by arrangement where cricket bats have been made for most of the world's great players since W. G Grace.

Bewl Bridge Reservoir, Flimwell
Largest inland lake in the South-East offering fishing, sailing, diving, windsurfing, rowing, bird-watching, and a nature-trail.

Saxons. A spell of fine weather in October is known as St Martin's Summer and this may have influenced the dedication.

Battle Abbey, a Benedictine house, was commenced in 1067 and was not consecrated until after William's death in 1094. The consecration was performed by Anselm, later St Anselm, then Archbishop of Canterbury; William's son, Rufus, presented William's great battle sword and coronation robes. The first abbot had already been appointed, and sixty monks were brought over from Marmoutier in Normandy to form the core of what was intended to be an establishment of 140. The high altar of the abbey was placed on the spot where

Harold fell, on the Conqueror's express instructions. (The monk William of Marmoutier wished to build lower down the hill, which was called Senlac from Santlache, meaning a sandy ridge.)

Battle Abbey had three parks, a vineyard, fishponds, and became the first commercial producer of cider in England. It was exempt from the jurisdiction of the bishop; it possessed the right of inquest, treasure trove, free warren, and the privilege of sanctuary. Its abbots were mitred and had a seat in governing councils which preceded parliament; they also had the right to pardon any criminal they met going to execution. The great gateway which dominates the town was built around 1338 by order of Abbot de Ketling as

part of fortifications licensed by Edward III in response to French raids on the coast. It is possible that the gatehouse was not completed until later than the ascribed date, due to outbreaks of the Black Death. The abbey was dissolved in 1538, becoming the property of Sir Anthony Browne, Master of the King's Horse.

The great battle took place on 14 October 1066; the Saxons occupying the hill where the abbey now stands. Harold's army had arrived on the previous day having force-marched from Stamford Bridge near York, where they had utterly defeated the army of Hardrada, King of Norway, and Harold's brother Tostig; both being slain.

Harold had hoped to surprise the Normans by an unexpected attack. He had rushed south in order to protect the area around Hastings, particularly his lands at Crowhurst and Whatlington, which were put to the sword. The spot chosen by Harold offered the best chance of defence. Standing astride the road to London, it was steep and protected by swamp, making it extremely difficult for the Norman cavalry to operate. It was also advantageous to the Saxon axe-men to be able to strike from a higher level.

William, encamped on Telham Hill, advanced to assault the Saxon shield wall. According to legend, the minstrel Taillefer rode between the armies throwing up and catching his lance, then hurling it into the Saxon ranks before rushing headlong into the attack. All

31

day long the battle raged with great slaughter on both sides. At one point the Normans broke and were pursued by the less disciplined Fyrd or irregular troops. Rallied by William, the Normans turned and cut down the Saxons when they reached the lower slopes, thus leaving a foothold on the hill. Much has been made of the 'feigned retreat' of the Normans, but it is unlikely that this tactic was unknown to an army feared throughout Europe, whereas a genuine retreat would be unmistakeable and would have tempted the Saxons to break ranks.

By evening, Harold, his brothers Gurth and Leofwine, and the house-carls or professional soldiers, weakened by a hail of arrows, had been cut down, and after a final stand in the Caldbec Hill area the remnants of the Saxon army made their escape.

The Bayeaux Tapestry is one of the few accounts we have of these times and it is worth studying. However, it is after all a piece of Norman propaganda. It does not for instance accept that Harold was forced to swear his oath to William.

Running down one side of the battlefield with an excellent view of the abbey and the twin towers of the apartments which Sir Anthony Browne hoped would be the home of Princess, later Queen, Elizabeth, is Powdermill Lane. The name commemorates the gunpowder mill which at its height manufactured over a ton of gunpowder a day. Always a hazardous trade, Battle residents made it even more dangerous by making gunpowder as a cottage industry and drying it in their ovens, with the inevitable explosions. These local disasters pale into insignificance when compared with one explosion at the powdermill which was heard at Lewes, twenty-five miles away. It has been said that the workers did not always have to get up and go to work — sometimes their work got up and came to them!

Battle church is a good one. Built between 1110 and 1125 by Abbot Ralph

The Old Pharmacy, Battle, dates from 1740

Mermaid Street, Rye

Water Street, Rye

Bodiam Castle

All Saint Street, Old Hastings

for the townsfolk, it has several brasses, some medieval painting, and a fine tomb of the afore-mentioned Sir Anthony Browne. The first timbered building near the abbey gateway is The Pilgrims Rest. Formerly the almonry of the abbey, it is a Wealden hall-house built around 1420, and as its name suggests it once served as a hostel for the pilgrims journeying to Sir Richard at Chichester or St Thomas à Becket in Canterbury.

Marley Lane in Battle leads to Sedlescombe, a pretty little village that once had a large ordnance factory and now provides a haven for the children of the Pestalozzi Village. In Sedlescombe during the nineteenth century, a hoard of coins was discovered. This was believed to be Harold's war-chest, never recovered after the battle.

Sedlescombe is one route to Bodiam Castle, which can also be reached from Robertsbridge. The castle at Bodiam was built by Sir Edward Dalyngrigge between 1385-90; during the Wars of the Roses it was surrendered to the Yorkists in 1483. It was the last castle to be built on traditional lines, because the advent of cannon rendered such buildings almost incapable of defence. Slighted by the parliamentary forces in 1643, the castle was almost entirely destroyed during the reign of Charles II. It was saved from total decay by Mad Jack Fuller in 1829, and in 1917 Lord Curzon carried out extensive repairs before presenting it to the nation in 1925. Bodiam Castle is now maintained by The National Trust and, standing in its moat, is the perfect fairytale castle. It is

A hammer pond at Ashburnham, near Battle: evidence of the Sussex iron industry

Bodiam Castle

possible to climb one of the towers and gaze down on the moat, and across to the river where tiles bearing the Classic Brittanicus stamp have been found.

The route from Sedlescombe to Rye winds through Northiam, Beckley and Peasmarsh following the old coastline. Northiam is a pretty little village of weather-boarded cottages, with two notable houses; Great Dixter and Brickwall, and one which is claimed to be the smallest in England. It stands, or more accurately crouches, at the end of the main street looking rather like Queen Mary's dolls house.

Great Dixter is one of the typically sympathetic restorations by Sir Edwin Lutyens, who added a complementary house from Benenden to the sixteenth-century timbered hall-house already

standing. Jointly with Nathaniel Lloyd, and with advice from Gertrude Jekyll, Lutyens also created the garden which under the expert eye of Nathaniel's son Christopher, an eminent gardening expert, is one of the show-pieces of the region.

Queen Elizabeth I slept at Brickwall when progressing to Rye as a guest of the Frewens, for many years a leading family in the area. Their monuments are in the church, and one of their number, with the thoroughly puritan name of Thankful Frewen, gave the communion table and altar rails in 1638. The family also produced an archbishop who was named Accepted. Brickwall is an impressive timbered house built in 1490, forty years after the native portion of Great Dixter. It is now a school but may

Great Dixter

be visited at certain times.

Beckley more or less merges with Northiam. It has a church mainly of the Decorated style, where there is an ancient chest dating from the twelfth century which was probably used to collect money for the crusades, and certainly for storing the church valuables. This is of a type known as a 'dug-out' chest made from a single tree trunk and often kept at the west side of the church.

Peasmarsh has a Norman church and a house called Peasmarsh Place, formerly home of the Liddell family of *Alice in Wonderland* fame.

The church at Playden contains a memorial to a Flemish brewer, Cornelis Roetmans, complete with beer barrels. This is a reminder that it was Huguenot and Flemish immigrants who brought hops and beer to this area, and to whom we owe the oast-houses of which there are numerous examples right through East Sussex and Kent.

Rye is arguably one of the most beautiful towns in Britain with its cobbled streets and timbered houses presenting a panorama of English history. Foreign sailors and smugglers rubbed shoulders in Mermaid Street, and the Watchbell has rung while torches burned the town and blood ran over the cobbles.

Julius Caesar found the inhabitants fierce and hostile, and this, allied to tenaciousness, bravery, and determination, has marked their hold upon this small outcrop. The name is an abbreviation of 'atter eye' or 'at the island'. It is uncertain when it first became a port of any significance, although it is possible that it was one of the outlets for the Roman iron trade around Northiam, Beckley, and Peasmarsh.

One of the great jokes among locals was always 'Peasmarsh Harbour', which being so far inland made it a Rye equivalent of Wigan Pier. However, in Roman times the sea did reach inland as far as Iden and also up the Tillingham valley. As Classis Brittanicus tiles have been found at Bodiam and Newenden, it is quite possible that the old joke is in fact a folk memory of real events and that the recession of the sea from the valleys of the Brede, Tillingham, and Rother made Rye into a port, as it was still by the sea.

Canute granted land, which included Rye, to the Abbey of Fécamp, and it remained under their sway until Henry III negotiated its return to crown governance. One part which was not returned in 1247 is still called Rye Foreign.

Rye became a member of the Cinque Ports Confederation in 1191, and established a mint in 1141. The Mint, leading from the High Street to the bottom of Mermaid Street, commemorates this. Although Rye possessed full Confederation privileges, it was at first a limb or sub-port of Hastings, but the town continued to prosper. Ypres Castle was built as part of other fortifications in 1249, and Rye received its charter of incorporation from Edward I in 1289. The elements also conspired to confer benefit on the town during this century. There was a terrible storm in 1287, when the sea flowed twice without ebbing; it totally destroyed nearby Winchelsea, and almost finished Hastings as a port, yet presented Rye with the River Rother which formerly reached the sea at New Romney. Effectively Rye became the only port fully in commission for many miles, and indeed the anchorage was improved.

By 1329 a wall was built around the town and the Landgate was completed. Another gate, Seagate, was also built at the bottom of Mermaid Street. Sometime around 1336 Rye became, with Winchelsea, a Head Port and the styling was changed to 'The Confederation of the Cinque Ports and Two Antient Townes'. Rye is therefore an 'Antient Towne' rather than a Cinque Port.

It is not certain why such a styling was chosen. Obviously there could not be seven Cinque Ports, which may be one outstanding reason, but why 'Antient' and why that spelling? It appears to be derived from a Latin root, possibly referring to a Roman Channel Fleet connection.

The Hundred Years' War led to a

series of raids and counter-raids across the channel by the Portsmen and their counterparts in France. Rye was attacked in 1339, but had recovered sufficiently to take part in the siege of Calais in 1347. More attacks followed in 1365, 1377, and 1448; the 1377 attack was particularly disastrous and only a handful of buildings survived. One of these, Baddyngs Tower, had to be sold to John de Ypres to raise money in 1430, so becoming known as Ypres Castle.

A petition was addressed to Richard II in 1378, entreating him 'to have consideration of the poor town of Rye, inasmuch as it has been several times taken and is unable further to repair the walls, wherefor the town is, on the sea side, open to enemies'. In fact Rye never truly recovered from the setbacks of this period, which also included outbreaks of the Black Death; and in 1449 Tenterden was made a limb of Rye to help share the burden, in the same way that Rye and Winchelsea were earlier bound to Hastings.

The sea began to recede during the fifteenth century and although Rye made a partial recovery, the decline in her fortunes began. Huguenots came and settled in the sixteenth century bringing new methods of boat-building, needle and clay-pipe making, silk and sail-making. Queen Elizabeth came in 1573 bringing the name 'Rye Royal'.

From that time until now the 'Antient Towne' has pursued its life quietly. It has been a Rotten Borough, with the Duke of Wellington as one of its two members. It has watched smugglers, kings, flying bombs, and tourists come and go. They have left their mark, but essentially Rye remains untouched; as G. K. Chesterton says, 'that wonderful inland island, crowned with a town as with a citadel, like a hill in a medieval picture'.

St Mary's church crowns that hill. Standing by Fletcher's House where dramatist John Fletcher, a contemporary of Shakespeare, was born in 1579, one looks up at the great Perpendicular window surmounted by the oldest turret clock in England, made by a Winchelsea man in 1562. Above the face stand the famous Quarterboys who strike the quarters, never the hours, on either side of a text from the Wisdom of Soloman. Inside the church, the clock has an 18ft pendulum, said to be made from the wreck of a Spanish ship.

Opposite Fletcher's House, the Town Hall (dating from 1742) contains many treasures, the chief of which are the town maces, two small Elizabethan maces and two large Georgian ones. The Mayor of Rye is also the King's Bailiff and so entitled to two maces. In 1767 two much more grand maces were presented to the town by three benefactors, one of whom was Mad Jack Fuller's grandmother. These maces were the model for the one used by the Canadian parliament.

The Town Hall also contains the gibbet irons complete with the skull of John Breads, a locally celebrated murderer. Breads, a butcher, had conceived a great hatred for the mayor, James Lamb, who had fined him for giving short weight. He plotted his revenge; lurking in the churchyard to waylay the mayor, he by mistake stabbed one Allan Grebell who was wearing Lamb's cloak. Breads then rushed about the town brandishing a bloodstained butchers knife and shouting in a drunken frenzy that 'Butchers should kill Lambs'. This, not unnaturally, was considered by the townsfolk to be a confession, and the 'sanguinary butcher' was tried and hanged on Gibbet Marsh near the windmill in 1744.

Mermaid Street contains the world famous Mermaid Inn, built in 1425. Here it was that the infamous Hawkhurst Gang sat drinking, their pistols on the table before them, with the Excise men powerless to curb their lawlessness. There have been many novels about the romance of smuggling, with the smugglers portrayed as devil-may-care rogues. The truth is somewhat different. One method the Hawkhurst

Augustinian Friary
Known as 'The Monastery' it was built around 1380. It stands in ancient Conduit Hill.

Church of St Mary
Twelfth-century church surmounted by the oldest working turret clock in Britain with a great pendulum which hangs down into the body of the church. The clock face is flanked by the famous Quarterboys. Known as the 'Cathedral of East Sussex'.

Lamb House (NT)
Eighteenth-century former home of authors Henry James and E. F. Benson.

Sound and Light Show
Imaginatively lit model with sound commentary telling the history of Rye.

Landgate
The last remaining town gate, dating from 1340.

Old Grammar School
Built in 1636 and immortalised by Thackeray in *Denis Duval.*

Mermaid Hotel
Smugglers' inn built in 1425, haunt of the notorious Hawkhurst Gang.

Town Hall
Built in 1743 and containing four exceptionally fine silver-gilt town maces, and gibbet irons containing the skull of a local murderer named Breads.

Ypres Castle
The principal fortification built by Peter of Savoy in 1250. Now houses an award winning museum.

gang employed to discipline informers was to nail them to their own front door, the romance of which escapes most people.

At the top of Mermaid Street stands Lamb House, home of the aforementioned Lamb family who were Mayors of Rye on seventy-eight occasions. It was built in 1723 and was the home of novelist Henry James during 1898-1916, and also of E. F. Benson whose 'Mapp and Lucia' books are enjoying such a vogue at the present time. George I stayed there briefly when forced ashore at Camber in 1726.

Other notable buildings are The Old Grammar School in the High Street, the Augustinian Friary known as The Monastery in Conduit Hill, (named from the waterpipes which ran down it) the Water House built by the church in

1735, and the house of The Friars of the Sack, a thirteenth-century building in Church Square.

The Landgate, part of the defences built in 1329, is similar in style to the Strandgate at Winchelsea; alongside it is the strangely named Turkeycock Lane. No doubt there is a prosaic reason for the name, but the ascribed reason is richly romantic. It seems that a monk or friar named Cantator had a very fine voice. By use of it and no doubt other blandishments, he had progressed far beyond what was considered seemly in an affair with a beautiful girl named Amanda. The two, after the fashion of the day, were buried alive for their sins, and Cantator's ghost was said to walk the area vainly trying to sing. Alas, earth and suffocation had reduced the fine voice to strangled noises reminiscent of a

St Mary's Church, Rye

turkey.

Oddly, as if to prove that all legend should be investigated to find if there is a core of truth, the South Eastern Railway workers came across two skeletons clasped in each other's arms. It must be pointed out, however, that one wealthy family in Rye bore the name Tokey!

The A259 to Winchelsea passes across what used to be a bay shared by the two towns. The bay was guarded by Camber Castle, built by Henry VIII in 1539. The castle can be reached by footpath either from the road to Rye Harbour or the road to Winchelsea Beach, although for several years now it has been closed for restoration.

Rye Harbour has a memorial to the crew of the *Mary Stanford*, which sank in full view of relatives with a loss of seventeen lives. It is sad to see how few surnames there are, and to reflect on the magnitude of such a disaster in a small community.

Winchelsea is the other 'Antient Towne', although not the original one which is supposed to lie somewhere off Rye Harbour. The original Winchelsea was a prosperous town supplying at one time ten ships to the Cinque Ports fleet. It was the principal cross channel port, and supplied England's first Admiral of the Fleet. But the sea on this coast is a fickle friend and a formidable enemy. Two great storms in 1250 and 1287 destroyed Old Winchelsea forever.

The inhabitants, alerted by the first storm, began to move up to Iham Hill, 'whereon only coneys did dwell', where Edward I had commenced a new town in 1272. This new town was planned on a grand scale, having thirty-nine squares of from one and a half to three acres each. The town was designed like the French 'Bastide' towns, and in fact the king brought over an architect from Bordeaux to supervise the project. Many of the squares were never actually built

Winchelsea

on, yet even so, in 1294 when Winchelsea supplied no fewer than thirteen ships out of an entire Cinque Ports fleet of fifty, it has been estimated that the population was between four and six thousand.

A constant motif along the coast of East Sussex has been the combined effects of the sea and the Hundred Years' War, and Winchelsea did not escape the attentions of either. The French sacked the town in 1359, 1380 and 1449. The sea was receding and by the end of the fifteenth century the twin enemies finally triumphed and Winchelsea ceased to be a port. When the diarist John Evelyn visited the once proud port he found it 'all in rubbish, and a few despicable hovels and cottages only standing'. That was in 1652, which shows how rapid was the decline.

The pride of Winchelsea is the church of St Thomas the Martyr, generally reckoned to be one of the best examples of the Decorated period in Britain. It is not certain whether the church was ruined by the French in 1449 or whether it was never completed. The date of its completion was about 1292, and it is possible that projected later phases were never undertaken due to French attacks, the gradually receding shore, and outbreaks of the terrible Black Death, which was rife during the fourteenth century.

The church was, or was intended to be, cruciform, but only the chancel with aisles and a ruined transept remain. Of special interest are the famous Alard tombs; one to Gervase Alard, first Admiral of the Fleet in England, and one to Stephen his grandson, also an Admiral in Edward II's reign. There are other tombs of persons unknown, believed to have been brought from Old Winchelsea, and there are crusaders' and palmers' crosses carved on several of the pillars, Winchelsea having been a principal embarkation port for crusaders.

Across the road from the church stands what is possibly the oldest building in Winchelsea. The Court Hall, now the local museum, is believed in part to have already been in existence when the removal to Iham Hill started. It has, like the museum in Rye, served as the town gaol and was at one time called The Water Bailiff's Prison. The Court Hall is the venue where for nearly 700 years the Mayor of Winchelsea has been elected every Easter Monday.

The Strand Gate is one of the original town gates, built late in the thirteenth century. The two other gates are the Pipe Well Gate, rebuilt in 1404, and the New Gate which is a mile from the town, giving some idea of the size of the original town plan.

New Gate is close to Hogs Hill windmill at Icklesham. This mill, which is the oldest in Sussex, was erected at Pett in 1670 and moved to its present site in 1790. For nearly three hundred years it has watched its sister mill across the A259 at Winchelsea, St Leonards Mill dating from 1703.

A Roman road has been recently discovered in Icklesham which seems to fit the proposition that there were Roman defences and port facilities between Pevensey and Hythe, as there is some evidence that there was a Roman port below the hill where St Leonards Mill now stands. Icklesham church, dedicated to St Nicholas, is Norman and suggests an area of greater importance than today.

Guestling was the meeting place for the Sussex Cinque Ports and again a Norman church bespeaks a former importance far beyond that suggested by the present scatter of houses. From the main road at Guestling Thorn, the low hills fall away gently to the River Brede, then rise again, thickly wooded, to where the B2089 takes the alternative route from Rye to Hastings, through Udimore and Brede, giving views of the whole of Rye Bay and even France on a clear day.

Udimore is said to have gained its name when the church was being built. Each night the stones were mysteriously

Church of St Nicholas, Icklesham
An architectural textbook of Norman and Early English styles.

Brickwall, Northiam
Beautiful timber-framed house with a chess garden. Home of the Frewen family for 300 years; Queen Elizabeth I once stayed here.

Great Dixter, Northiam
Timber-framed manor house restored by Sir Edwin Lutyens who also designed the garden, famous for its topiary, yew hedges, and flower borders.

Cherries Folk Museum, Playden
Aspects of local life and work before 1946.

Rye Harbour Nature Reserve
An area of marsh, shingle, river, and shore with a hide for visitors. Rare birds include avocets, and osprey.

Camber Castle
Can be reached by a footpath which runs from the road to Rye Harbour, or from Sea Road, Winchelsea Beach. A fort built in 1539 by Henry VIII to protect the entrance to the joint harbour of Rye and Winchelsea.

Church of St Thomas, Winchelsea
Considered to be the best example of Decorated work in Sussex. Contains the famous tombs of the Alards, England's first admirals.

Court Hall, Winchelsea
Once a prison, now a museum, this building in part pre-dated the town.

St Leonards Mill, Winchelsea (NT)
Sweepless body of a post mill built about 1700.

Strand Gate, Winchelsea
Thirteenth-century gateway, one of three in the town. Superb views over Romney Marsh.

---

moved and a voice whispered in the wind 'O'er the mere, o'er the mere. . .' When the hint was taken the interruptions ceased. Whether it was the spirit of Uda the Saxon, whose mere it was, is not known. It is known, however, that from this ridge Queen Phillippa watched the English Fleet under the command of her husband and son, Edward III and the Black Prince, destroy a Spanish pirate fleet off Winchelsea in 1341.

Brede stands on the road from Hastings to Tenterden near its junction with the B2089 at Broad Oak. Iron has been worked there at least since Roman times, and cannons were made there almost since ordnance was first cast. Clare Sheridan, the sculptress, lived at historic Brede Place, now happily to be restored after a disastrous fire, and a Madonna carved by her stands in the church, together with a cradle in which Dean Swift slept as a baby. The church, the parish church of St George, is Early English, dating from around 1200.

A Brede resident who could have done with some professional help with his image was Sir Goddard Oxenbridge. Sir Goddard was reputed to be a devourer of children who could not be killed by metal. The children of Sussex got him drunk and then sawed him in half with a wooden saw at a place known, not surprisingly, as Groaning Bridge.

Westfield straggles along the road for what seems to be a long time. The church is Norman with two squints, and the area once belonged to Battle Abbey. The road continues into Hastings past several rather nice little oast-houses before joining the A21 at Baldslow, where it is also possible to skirt around Hastings via The Ridge and re-enter the Old Town.

2 From Pevensey to Lewes

Like Winchelsea, Pevensey was stranded when the sea ebbed and never returned. With it went the importance vested in a member of the Cinque Ports Confederation which gave Pevensey a mayor, a mint, a court, and a town hall; however even the sea cannot rob this ancient spot of its history.

There seems to be no record of any occupation of Pevensey before Roman times; they built the fort or castle of *Anderida* somewhere around AD340, as part of a chain of defence known as the Forts of the Saxon Shore. The walls of the fort are over 12ft thick, with a core of flint rubble, faced with small stones. There is a plinth of green sandstone and three string courses, the upper one of brick. The walls enclose an area of some ten acres in an oval configuration, with ten bastion towers on which would have been mounted ballista (a kind of giant crossbow). Dominating the haven of Pevensey from a promontory by the entrance, the fort with its garrison of some thousand marines would have presented insuperable problems for any Saxon raiding party.

Recently, it has been suggested that the Saxon Shore Forts were built to keep out not Saxons but Romans. There is some evidence that Carausius, who was Commander of the Roman Fleet, rebelled against Rome and staged a coup with himself as Emperor in AD288, which was successful to the extent that it was many years before Rome was able to regain control; these forts deterring Rome until a strong enough force could be mustered.

This interesting theory, however, seems to show a lack of the practical common sense that such a commander would need. It is far more likely that Rome ordered the building of the Saxon Shore Forts to counter raids which had already started in the third century AD. Fishbourne was destroyed by such a raid in AD270. This would account for the name 'Forts of the Saxon Shore', with their commander bearing the title 'Count of the Saxon Shore', and for the standardised design.

Furthermore, to rebel against Rome before defences, which would take several years to build, had even been started, thus risking a punitive attack as soon as the senate heard the news, would have been foolish. To sieze power once the forts were completed would have been much wiser. This would place the building of *Anderida* nearer to the sometimes quoted date of AD250 making it exactly contemporary with the forts at Richborough, Lympne and Porchester.

When Honorius ordered the legions to leave Britain, the Romano-British in the area used the castle to defend themselves against increasing Saxon raids. In 491, however, a Saxon chief, Aella, besieged *Anderida* and slaughtered every Briton in the area. According to the *Anglo-Saxon Chronicle* this was after a six-month siege, when the Saxons were infuriated by the long resistance and the heavy losses they suffered. It is said that the Saxons would never thereafter live within the castle because of the dark deeds done that day, and they therefore established the village that still exists.

William the Conqueror landed here in 1066, by tradition at Normans Bay. It is stated in a number of books that his fleet was heading for Hastings and was blown astray, but several factors make this unlikely. The Bayeaux Tapestry, for example, nowhere depicts any difficulty in embarkation, the voyage, or the landing, which would have been portrayed to William's credit as another

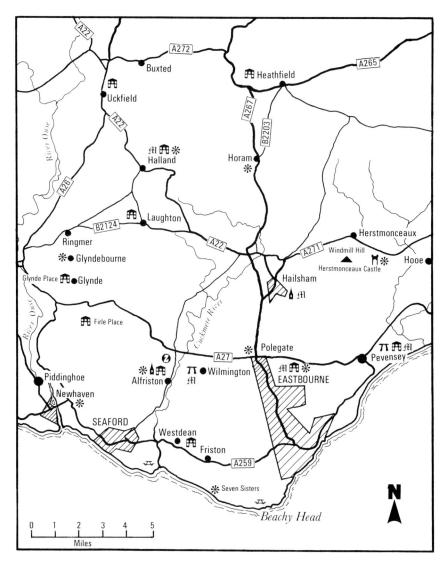

obstacle overcome. Furthermore, the
Norman fleet, heavily loaded with men,
had been waiting for, and needed,
favourable winds. One must conclude,
therefore, that they sailed advisedly,
knowing the wind to be suitable for their
purpose.

Secondly, William would have been
well aware of the existence of this fort
and harbour as it was already an
important port for cross channel trade

to France and Flanders, and it had
belonged to the Abbey of St Denis at
Paris. Thirdly, William was almost
certainly unaware of the attack by
Hardrada in the north and would have
expected fierce opposition. In these
circumstances, a frontal assault on
Hastings would be utterly stupid. How
much better to establish a bridgehead
with an immediately defensible fortress,
which would enable him to ascertain the

44

The North Wall, Pevensey Saxon Shore fort

position and strength of the Saxon forces.

This strategy certainly worked; the Norman fleet were able to land unopposed and to obtain provisions, after which they marched to Hastings and took it with little difficulty.

In 1068 William placed the castle at Peovensels, as it was then known, in the charge of the Earl of Mortaigne, the first Norman Baron of Hastings. In the following year, building operations commenced on the Norman castle which were to continue, on and off, until 1245. Work was also done to repair the Roman structure, and a mint was established in 1075, which issued coins during the reign of William I, William II, and Stephen. The present Old Mint House, built in 1343, occupies the same site.

Unlike some castles in the area, Pevensey Castle saw considerable service. In 1088 William Rufus beseiged it and starved out Bishop Odo and Robert de Mortaigne who were supporters of Duke Robert's claim to the throne. In 1246 it passed to Peter of Savoy, builder of Ypres Castle in Rye, and in 1372 it was given to John of Gaunt.

On the accession of Henry IV, Sir John Pelham was created Constable of the Castle. In 1399 when Sir John was assisting Henry, Duke of Lancaster to regain the throne, his wife, Lady Joan, successfully defended the castle against attacks by supporters of the deposed King Richard. It was also besieged by King Stephen and by Simon de Montfort.

In the fifteenth century, Pevensey Castle was a prison for three distinguished prisoners: Edward, Duke of York in 1405; Prince James, later James I of Scotland, in 1418; and Joan of Navarre in 1419. The castle remained a fortress until the reign of Elizabeth I, and there is still a culverin of that date which bears her initials and the Tudor rose. But perhaps the most evocative artefact of all is a Roman soldier's grave. Looking down at the stone and remembering all soldiers who have died on foreign shores seems to make the Romans very real and very human.

The tiny Court House in the main street was also the Town Hall, claiming to be the smallest in England. It was built in 1542 and also served as a prison, with two cells. The chief magistrate had the power to impose the death penalty and the prisoners had the power to choose whether they were hanged or drowned. This sentence, plus whipping for many non-capital offences (the convict was tied to a cart and whipped to the scene of the crime), could account for there only being two cells. The building is now a museum and is proud possessor of the oldest existing Cinque Ports seal.

Pevensey was an incorporated borough in the Confederation of the Cinque Ports and was a limb of Hastings. The date of its attachment to Hastings is uncertain but it is likely to have been early in the thirteenth century, although it could have been as a result of the damage suffered by Hastings in the two storms of 1250 and 1287.

The Old Mint House was, between 1542 and 1549, the home of Andrew Borde, who was physician to Henry VIII

and the original 'Merry Andrew'. He owned some land near Pevensey known as Gotham, and wrote a book *'Tales of the Mad Men of Gotham'* satirising the townspeople of his day. He swore that the chief magistrate once sentenced an eel to death by drowning, and on another occasion found a man guilty of manslaughter for stealing a pair of breeches.

Pevensey has several Martello Towers, which were built to protect England from Napoleon; a long chain of forts stretched from Seaford almost into Folkestone. They are about 40ft in diameter at the base tapering to 30ft at the top, two storeys high, with walls from 5ft to 12ft thick, so that those adapting them for habitation have had some difficulty putting in windows. They were built as gun-towers and carried a twenty-four pounder swivel gun, and a 5in howitzer. There are two versions of how they came by their name. The most commonly accepted is that they are named after a similar type of fort which in 1794 gave the British considerable trouble at Mortella Point on the North-West coast of Corsica. The second, lesser known theory, is that they were designed by Horatio Martelli who is buried at St Clements, Hastings.

Both St Nicholas' church at Pevensey (which dates roughly from 1150-1300) and St Mary's church at Westham (1080-1300) are very well worth visiting, as

they exemplify much of interest.

At the eastern end of the Pevensey rape is an area which has for various reasons seen great changes, although the recession of the sea and the decline of Hastings were the greatest. Much of Hooe has vanished; so have Northeye and Hydneye which were limbs of Hastings. Hooe church still stands and nearby Court Lodge is a fine seventeenth-century manor house. Wartling is a tiny, pretty village on the edge of the levels.

The old shoreline is followed by the A271, passing through Herstmonceux. Here, at Herstmonceux Castle, is the

---

PLACES OF INTEREST IN AND AROUND PEVENSEY

Pevensey Castle (DoE)
Roman castle with an added Norman keep, dating originally from around AD 250.

Old Mint House, Pevensey
Former home of Andrew Borde, the original 'Merry Andrew'. Now antique showrooms occupy this lovely timbered house.

Court House, Pevensey
Smallest town hall in Britain, containing an interesting museum.

Herstmonceux Castle, home of the Royal Observatory

home of the Observatory formerly at
Greenwich. The castle, built in 1440 by
Sir Roger de Fiennes, is unusual in that
it is built of Flemish brick which was not
generally introduced until a hundred
years later. The introduction of the
cannon had rendered the castle
redundant in warfare, and
Herstmonceux reflects this, as it is
principally a mansion house with
notional rather than practical defences.
It is said that in its finished state it had a
window for every day of the year and a
chimney for every Sunday. It was
considerably reduced in size in 1777 and
stood as a picturesque, ivy-covered ruin
until it was restored in 1913. During the
time that it was unoccupied it became a
dropping point for smuggled cargoes,
which was why a legend of a headless
drummer which haunted the castle was

invented. All over England smugglers,
who had a natural objection to being
watched while at work, invented
apparitions to frighten the locals and
keep them indoors at night. Legions of
headless horsemen, phantom coaches,
evil monks and ghastly women moaned,
clanked chains, and appeared wherever
smugglers plied their trade. The
smugglers of Herstmonceux, probably
the Alfriston Gang, were of a more
histrionic bent and invented a 9ft high
headless drummer to patrol the
battlements.

The castle, and Herstmonceux Place
just outside the park at one time
belonged to the Hare family of whom
Augustus, who wrote *Memorials of a
Quiet Life,* was the most famous. One of
his ancestors, Georgiana Hare Naylor,
was a claimant to the title of leading

Sussex eccentric, riding in the park on a donkey, dressed in a white shift, and attending church accompanied by a white doe.

It is a great pity that the castle is not more fully open to the public, being closed but for two small rooms containing exhibitions. If the Royal Observatory ever choose to open it fully it will become a major attraction.

The other famous Herstmonceaux institution is a kind of gardening basket known as the 'Sussex Trug' which is famous the world over. Introduced some 140 years ago, the trug achieved great success at the Great Exhibition in 1851. The founder of the firm (which still proudly bears his name), Thomas Smith, walked to London with the baskets and attracted the notice of Queen Victoria. The trugs are boat-shaped, made from laths of willow; the name is derived from the Saxon *trog* meaning boat-shaped.

Herstmonceux church, All Saints, is Transitional and contains a brass of 1402 to William Ffiennes, and the famous Dacre Monument (the Fiennes family were also the Lords Dacre), which was also intended to serve as an Easter Sepulchre. There is a fine yew tree in the churchyard, and a fourteenth-century tithe barn close by.

Just along the road towards Ninfield is Windmill Hill, where a large post mill, possibly eighteenth century, presents a

sad sight mouldering away clad in rusty corrugated iron.

Hellingly has a Saxon churchyard and a moated grange called Horselunges Manor, a beautiful timbered building.

North of Herstmonceux one re-enters the Weald and iron country. Heathfield had a famous gun foundry which operated until 1787 and the former hammerpond is now a garden. It is at Heathfield that spring officially starts. An old woman comes to the 'Heffle Fair' and releases the first cuckoo from her basket, after which spring is allowed to commence.

Natural gas was found at Heathfield in 1895, and for many years was used to light the station and the street outside. In these days when oil prospecting is taking place all over Sussex that must be an encouragement to the survey teams if not to the inhabitants.

Heathfield Park, built in 1767 on an earlier site, was the home of General Elliott, later Lord Heathfield, who successfully held Gibraltar against a Franco-Spanish siege during 1779-83. The Gibraltar Tower was erected in memory of the general and this feat. It is worth mentioning here, for the benefit of those with old or unrevised guide books, that there is no wildlife park at Heathfield Park and there has not been for several years.

Both Cross-In-Hand and Punnetts

The traditional 'Sussex Trug'

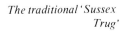

The Watermill, Michelham Priory

Town possess windmills. Cross-In-Hand mill is the largest post mill in Sussex. It started life at Uckfield in 1806, and last worked commercially in 1969. Punnetts Town mill is known variously as Blackdown Mill and Cherry Clack Mill — this last because it started life in a cherry orchard at Biddenden, being erected on the present site in 1856.

Horam is the home of the Merrydown Company, who offer wine tours, and one can also buy their famous '1066' elderflower wine.

Cade Street is the spot where Jack Cade the rebel was fatally wounded by Alexander Iden, Sheriff of Kent. Warbleton is the site where the Hastings Priory monks, driven away by the sea, found a new home on ground donated by Sir John Pelham in 1406. The priory remains now form part of Priory Farm.

Hailsham is a market town which was granted its market charter in 1252. Rope has been made in Hailsham for many years, including the ropes used at executions.

About two miles from Hailsham, Michelham Priory stands in beautiful grounds surrounded by a moat. Built by Gilbert de Aquila in 1229, this was an Augustinian house but apparently not a dedicated one for in 1283 fines were imposed for non-residence and other offences. In 1441 they were breaking silence and visiting taverns, and were still doing so in 1478. In 1302 Edward I spent a night at Michelham while en route to Battle Abbey. The impressive gatehouse was added in 1385 and the priory was dissolved in 1536.

The Long Man of Wilmington

Michelham Priory is now in the care of the Sussex Archaeological Trust and the public can see furniture, tapestries, toys, a fascinating collection of musical instruments, farm wagons, and a blacksmith's and wheelwright's museum. In addition there are many events every year, including one of the best craft fairs in England. The priory adjoins Abbots Wood which has nature trails and picnic sites.

Heading on towards Brighton on the A27, The Long Man of Wilmington can be seen on the left, and by going through Wilmington it is possible to park and walk up to the chalk giant outlined on Windover Hill. How he got there no-one knows and who he is no-one can say. He has been ascribed to the ancient Britons, the Romans, the Saxons, and the Vikings. He has variously been claimed as Hercules, Woden, Baldur (a Norse god), or a Celtic god throwing open the doors of heaven to admit the sun. He has even been described as an eighteenth-century joke.

One theory which perhaps merits closer examination is that the Long Man represents a pilgrim cut to advertise to pilgrims that accommodation was available at nearby Wilmington Priory.

Certainly the monks would have had the time, the education and the support to undertake the work. Monks would be used to illustrating manuscripts and planning buildings, and the workers would have others to grow crops and provide food so that the project could progress unhindered.

By the time Wilmington Priory was established, there was an extensive pilgrim traffic between Canterbury (St Thomas), Chichester (St Richard), and Winchester (St Swithin), which certainly used the South Downs Way past the priory for parts of the journey. It is well known among Downsmen that when caught by fog in that area one must find the Long Man. If one then walks straight down his body one arrives at the priory and so the village. This makes the Long Man both a directional and an advertising sign, an eminently practical expedient.

Wilmington Priory is now an agricultural museum run by the Sussex Archaeological Trust and its curator is also custodian of the Long Man. It was originally established in 1088, although the present building dates from about 1243, by an alien Benedictine order, a cell of the Norman Abbey of Grestein.

Alfriston Old Clergy House

They were regarded with suspicion during the Hundred Years' War, and the priory was seized by Richard II in 1380 and suppressed in 1414.

Alfriston was another smuggling town. E. V. Lucas goes as far as to say that smuggling was Alfriston's industry. Cuckmere Haven, close by, offered ideal conditions and Mad Jack Fuller's contribution of a lighthouse on Beachy Head, Belle Tout, built in 1831, probably helped them at least as much as it helped mariners. Stanton Collins, the leader of the Alfriston Gang, lived in Market Cross House, now called the Smugglers Inn.

The Star Inn was a pilgrims' inn before it was a haunt of smugglers. It appears to be contemporary with The Pilgrims Rest at Battle and The Mermaid in Rye; that is to say, dating from around 1420. If indeed Wilmington Priory was providing accommodation, then its closure in 1414 would have created the need for alternative arrangements close by and The Star could have been built for that reason.

The Old Clergy House stands near the church. Thatched, timbered, and beautiful, it is a pre-reformation priests' house of about 1350, now owned by the National Trust. It was the first house they acquired, in 1896, for £10. The shop is a very good one which opens briefly for Christmas shopping even though the house is closed. A number of National Trust properties do this.

The open space where the church stands is called The Tye, a scene of wondrous events when the church was being built. Not only did invisible hands keep dismantling the stone-work and moving the stones to the present site, but white oxen were discovered lying in a cruciform formation to inform the builders what shape was required. As the church of St Andrew is built on its mound in the shape of a cross, one must presume that the masons had heard of Udimore and bowed to the inevitable.

St Andrew's was completed at about the same time as the Clergy House, possibly on the site of an earlier church. It is called the 'Cathedral of the Downs', not for its grandeur but for its size compared with most Downland churches. Lullington nearby for instance is only 16ft square.

South of Alfriston lie Friston Forest and the Seven Sisters Country Park. The forest is a Forestry Commission property where deciduous trees have

51

been protected by conifers which are being removed. Seven Sisters Country Park is an area of downland marsh, and chalk cliff, containing the much photographed meanders of the River Cuckmere. The centre for the park, sited in a barn opposite the car park, is excellent and now also contains 'The Living World' an additional insect and shore life exhibition.

Charleston Manor is at West Dean. It is at present only possible to visit the gardens, which are in traditional English style created by Sir Oswald and Lady Birley in the 1930s and extremely attractive. The house was constructed at different times and shows examples of styles ranging from Norman to Georgian, and possesses a fine tithe barn and dovecot.

Charleston Manor is not to be confused with Charleston Farm, which gained its fame by connection with the Bloomsbury set. The farm lies west of Selmeston and was the home of Vanessa Bell, who was visited by her sister Virginia Woolf, and by Keynes, T. S. Eliot, Bertrand Russell, Lytton Strachey and Benjamin Britten among others. The Bloomsbury group were influenced by the philosopher, G. E. Moore and took their attitudes from his statement that 'the rational ultimate end of human progress consists in the pleasures of human intercourse and the enjoyment of beautiful objects'.

Seaford was a limb of Hastings in the Cinque Ports Confederation, although the church is the only remaining link with that period. There is once again a Roman connection, for a Roman cemetery was discovered on Seaford Head, that majestic headland that gazes down on the Seven Sisters to the east. From west to east the Seven Sisters are called: Haven Brow, Short Brow, Rough Brow, Brass Point, Flagstaff Point, Baily's Brow, and West Hill Brow.

Seaford became a limb of Hastings in 1229, and by 1347 it was contributing five ships and eighty men to the Cinque Ports Fleet. However, after a storm in

Glynde Place

1579 diverted the Ouse, the little village of Meeching became Newhaven and all port activity at Seaford ceased. Of Newhaven, E. V. Lucas in *Highways and Byways in Sussex* contributes the following; 'Of Newhaven there is little to say, except that in rough weather the traveller from France is very glad to reach it, and on a fine day the traveller from England is happy to leave it behind.' However, a more interesting aspect of Newhaven is Fort Newhaven which was commenced in 1864 and completed in 1870. It was designed to protect this part of the coast from attack from the continent. After the coastal artillery was disbanded in 1956 the fort lay derelict until 1981, when it was restored.

Bishopstone has a Saxon church with a Saxon sundial over the porch bearing the name 'Eadric'. This venerable church radiates peace and wonder, and great simplicity.

52

Firle Place

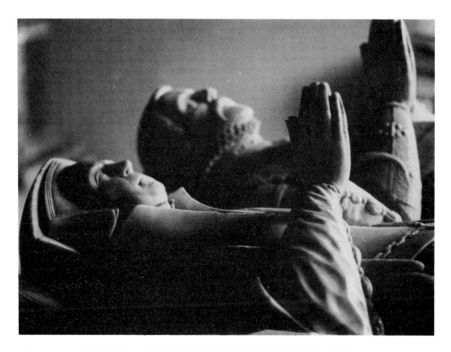

Monuments in Firle Church

North of Alfriston, Drusillas Zoo offers all kinds of small, furry or woolly animals that little children love. There is a shop, a bakery, crafts, a garden centre, a small railway, an adventure playground, and more. There is also the Valley Wine Cellars and a cider museum, where wine and cider festivals are held in the autumn.

Glynde Place was built around 1560 for William Morley, whose descendent Herbert was one of the judges at the trial of Charles I, but refused to sign the death warrant. The house was rebuilt by Richard Trevor, Bishop of Durham, in 1752 and is famous for its paintings by Rubens, Zoffany, Hoffner, and Lely, fine needlework, and rare bronzes.

Nearby Firle Place was built much earlier in 1475, but like Glynde Place it was remodelled around 1730 incorporating the Tudor house. It has been the home of the Gage family for 500 years from the time that John Gage built the original house. Another John was ward of the Duke of Buckingham and accompanied Henry VIII on his French expedition in 1513, later becoming comptroller of Calais. Later still he was to be Constable of the Tower of London during the imprisonment of Lady Jane Grey. Sir Edward Gage was the Sheriff of Sussex who supervised the burning of the Lewes martyrs, and General Thomas Gage was Governor of Massachusetts.The family was responsible for introducing greengages into this country.

There are pictures by Fra Bartolommeo, Correggio, Guardi, Reynolds, Van Dyke and many besides; Louis Quinze and Louis Seize furniture, Sèvres porcelain, and so many other priceless pieces in this beautiful Sussex treasure house standing in parkland beneath Firle Beacon. Everyone should visit Firle and Glynde, both open on Mondays. This is the gentle face of Sussex, the beauty of rolling downs and timeless fields which caused Kipling to write:

'Here through the strong and shadeless days
The tinkling silence thrills
Or little, lost Down churches praise
The Lord who made the hills'

Glyndebourne has the famous opera house which brings the same qualities of civilisation and beauty to the ear that the scenery brings to the eye. The opera house was opened in 1934 for John Christie.

Ringmer, which has always been closely associated with Glyndebourne, possesses a huge village green where ladies' teams play a sort of cross between cricket and netball called stoolball, a game which seems confined to Kent and Sussex. The wicket is like a netball stand without the net, and the bat like a large, thick table tennis bat with a long handle.

Gilbert White of Selborne, the famous naturalist, visited his aunt here and immortalised her tortoise Timothy in his work, *The Natural History of Selborne.* William Penn the Quaker and founder of Pensylvania married Gulielma Springett of Ringmer and John Harvard, founder of the American university, also married a Ringmer girl.

Neighbouring Laughton was the home of the Pelhams whose history is so interwoven with Sussex. Sir John Pelham captured the King of France at Poitiers and was granted the buckle from his swordbelt, which was adopted as the Pelham crest. Many buildings bear his badge, which is like a capital letter A with an additional vertical line from the crosspiece to the apex. The Pelhams lived at Laughton Place of which only the tower, dating from 1534, remains.

North of Laughton the Bentley Wildfowl Reserve and Motor Museum is at Halland. It was formerly the home and collection of Gerald Askew, and was presented to East Sussex County Council by his widow in 1978 as a memorial. The Askews converted the original Tudor farmhouse into a Palladian-style residence, commissioning Raymond Erith, who restored 10 and 11 Downing Street in

The Motor Museum, Bentley

London. The house is now very reminiscent of the Pavilion at Brighton, particularly the morning room and the Chinese room. The Philip Rickman gallery contains a number of wildfowl paintings by this well-known Sussex artist.

The truly beautiful gardens lead to the wildfowl reserve where there are more than a thousand birds of over a hundred species. Some of the birds have names that defy belief. Armed with the excellent guidebook see if you can locate the Bufflehead, the Canvasback, the Flightless Steamer Duck, the Hottentot Teal, and the Pied Ne-Ne. Do not miss the Whistling Tree Duck, and be sure to listen to the cackling Canada Goose. Recently the stables have been adapted to house a collection of vintage cars along with a few veteran vehicles.

Arlington has a reservoir with nature trails, a stock-car and banger-racing stadium, and in the spring a local farm opens up its Bluebell Walk, which when they are in full bloom, seem to make the air around them vibrate with colour.

The largest town in the Pevensey Rape has many names. It has been called Suntrap of the South, a queen of watering places, and the Entertainment Capital of the South. Eastbourne is all of these and more; a conference centre with the best floral displays in Europe, an excellent shopping centre, and a well situated base for touring.

Although Eastbourne is old there is little of its early history to be seen today. The old town has a fine old church, St Mary, which dates from the twelfth century; the Lamb Inn is probably fourteenth century; there is a sixteenth-century parsonage, and several other old buildings including the Towner Gallery, which has a large collection of the works of British artists and stages many

East Dean

temporary exhibitions.

Eastbourne was already a fashionable resort when the chief landowner and lord of the manor, the Duke of Devonshire, began to develop the town during the 1850s and 1860s. Everywhere in the town there are names associated with the Devonshires. Names such as Cavendish, Compton, Hartington, Devonshire and Chatsworth, all recall the man who did so much to establish Eastbourne as a top resort.

The three-mile seafront with its terraced parades and gardens with fountains, is a picture. No shops clutter the front, and at night with the lights illuminating the flowers and filling the fountains with a million highlights, it is even more strikingly beautiful.

Four landmarks punctuate the seafront. To the east, the Great

Redoubt, a Napoleonic fort built in 1804-12, contains the Sussex Combined Services Museum. Moving westwards the next landmark is the pier, over a thousand feet long with all the traditional diversions. At the centre of Grand Parade is the Bandstand, and then finally the Wish Tower 73, a martello tower that has recently had its cannon restored, and houses the Coastal Defence Museum. Under the Wish Tower stands the first permanent Lifeboat Museum.

Two fairly recent additions to the wide range of entertainment are Treasure Island and the Butterfly Centre; this last being a semi-tropical enclosed area with exotic plants, waterfalls, and landscaped gardens, where many breeds of butterfly fly free. Treasure Island is a children's

The 'Carpet Gardens', Eastbourne

The Front, Eastbourne

Beachy Head
World famous beauty spot and one end of the South Downs Way. Intepretation centre with leaflets.

The Butterfly Centre, Royal Parade
Butterflies flying free amid landscaped gardens with waterfalls and exotic plants.

The Lifeboat Museum, Green Parade
First permanent lifeboat museum in the country.

The Redoubt, Royal Parade
Napoleonic fort offering displays of coastal defence and Sussex Combined Services.

Wish Tower 73
Martello Tower with coastal defence displays.

Towner Art Gallery
Gallery in an old manor house with pictures of many of Britain's leading painters of the eighteenth and nineteenth centuries, plus regular exhibitions.

playground with huge fibreglass animals, a pirate ship, all sorts of paddling pools and sand pits, and a range of climbing ropes, swings, see-saws, and slides. It won an award for its originality when it was built.

Between Grand Parade and the beach to the west of the pier are the Carpet Gardens where there is always a brilliant display of flowers arranged in carpet patterns. Continuing to the west, the front leads to Beachy Head. It is possible to drive to Beachy Head up a twisting, tree-enclosed road, or walk up the footpath which is the start of the South Downs Way, and which continues for some ninety miles to Buriton in Hampshire.

This magnificent headland rises sheer from the sea 536ft above the lighthouse, built in 1902. From the top of the cliff the view is wide-ranging and superb; anything up to sixty miles on a clear day. Beachy is thought to derive from the French, 'beau chef' meaning beautiful headland. As beautiful as it is, it is most unwise to walk too close to the edge, as it is very prone to crumbling. The only person known to have survived a fall is a commando who fell over the edge during a World War II training exercise. A well-known landmark in the area is Mad Jack Fuller's lighthouse, 'Belle Tout'. No-one has yet explained

satisfactorily the derivation of the name. Both Swinburne and Richard Jeffries loved Beachy Head as did Lewis Carroll. Perhaps also some of the dream-like qualities of Debussy's music were born on these heights while he was living in Eastbourne.

Walkers and naturalists will find this area one of the most interesting in the county, containing as it does Wealden, marsh, and Downland habitats. The opportunities to study a wide range of flora and fauna are correspondingly greater. There are two 'interpretation' centres in this area; at Seven Sisters Country Park and at Beachy Head.

The Downland areas are rich in chalkland plant life, with trefoils and vetches, wayfaring trees, rampions and scarlet pimpernel. More than forty-five species have been recorded in Seven Sisters Country Park including early purple, common spotted, and pyramidal orchids. Five different blue butterflies can be found in this area, and Beachy Head and Seaford Head are observation points for migrating birds.

On Pevensey Levels wintering birds include snipe, golden plover, redshanks, and in the summer sedge and reed warblers abound. In this area swallows and martins still arrive in great numbers, as do buntings, redstarts and wagtails. The area is rich in insect life and many

Polegate Mill

types of dragonflies and damsel flies can ben seen on the levels and in the Cuckmere Valley.

In the woodlands back in the Weald, all three British woodpeckers can be seen. The green woodpecker is called the yaffle in Sussex, and its laughing call is a signal of wet weather. There are also tree-creepers and nuthatches, and many of the noisy but usually invisible jays.

Clergy House, Alfriston (NT)
First acquisition of the National
Trust in 1896. A timber-framed and
thatched building of great charm,
with an Elizabethan knot-garden.

Drusillas, Afriston
A children's zoo with much that is
soft and cuddly, plus a small railway
and an adventure playground. Also
incorporating Valley Wine Cellars.

Buckleys Shop Museum, Polegate
A nostalgic Victorian-Edwardian
shop with a traditional tearoom.

Polegate Windmill
A tower mill of 1817 with a museum
devoted to milling.

Charleston Manor, near Seaford
A beautiful traditional English
country garden.

**Seven Sisters Country Park, near
Seaford**
Nearly 700 acres of chalkland
habitat.

The Living World, near Seaford
In the Seven Sisters interpretation
centre displaying scorpions, hairy
spiders, stick insects and other things
that creep and crawl.

Michelham Priory, Upper Dicker
Augustinian Priory of 1229 with
good furniture and a musical
instrument collection. There is a
working watermill in the grounds.

Long Man of Wilmington
Giant chalk figure, enigmatic and
mysterious, 230ft tall.

Wilmington Priory
Agricultural museum in ancient
surroundings near the Long Man.

Kestrels, sparrowhawks, hobbies, marsh
harriers, and buzzards are present, and
ospreys have recently been seen at local
reservoirs. There has also been a
reported sighting of a red kite.

All the native owls are common in this
region as are several varieties of bat, and
it is still possible in some places to
simultaneously listen to nightingales and
look at glow-worms. Happily some
species of hawk moth are making a
recovery along the south coast and it is
possible to see the hummingbird
hawkmoth hovering in front of flowers
even in domestic gardens, while both the
privet and elephant hawk moths appear
to be gaining in numbers.

3 From Lewes to Brighton and Hove

Lewes is the county town of East Sussex and occupies a spur of the South Downs to the west of the River Ouse, at a point where it flows through a narrow gap in the chalk hills.

This area has been inhabited since very early times as the extensive hill fort on Mount Caburn testifies. The Romans certainly recognised the importance of the site, and established a camp, thought by some historians to be *Mutuantonis*, to guard one of their lines of communication northwards. This camp was built on the site subsequently occupied by the castle.

By Saxon times Lewes had developed into a centre of great importance, possessing two mints in the time of Edward the Confessor. Remains of a Saxon cemetery were discovered at Saxonbury at the western end of Southover High Street.

After the Conquest William gave this Rape to his son-in-law William de

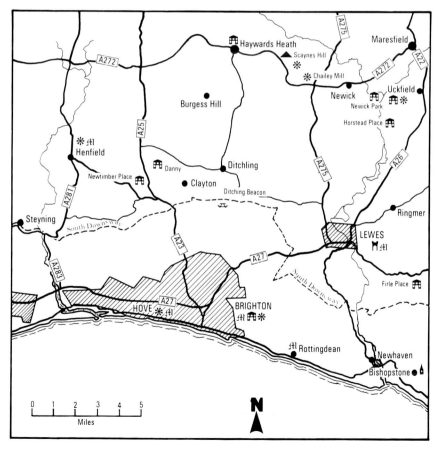

Warenne who was married to Gundrada. It was he who commenced the building of the present castle in 1078 and improvements were made by members of the same family up to the building of the massive barbican around 1330. The view from the keep of Lewes Castle is positively eagle-like, and well worth the climb. Southwards it encompasses the Ouse valley as far as Newhaven, to the east to Firle, and westwards to Mount Harry.

On the slopes of Mount Harry in 1264, Simon de Montfort and the barons defeated Henry III at the Battle of Lewes. The treaty signed at the conclusion of this battle was called The Mise of Lewes, and it marked the beginning of parliamentary government in England.

Henry III was taking refuge in the Cluniac Priory at Lewes before the battle, after a number of encounters with Simon de Montfort's forces in the Midlands. The priory had been built by William de Warenne as a result of an expiatory pilgrimage to Rome in 1076. During this pilgrimage de Warenne and Gundrada sheltered at the monastery of St Per at Cluny, and were treated so hospitably that upon returning to Lewes they commenced building the Priory of St Pancras, where they were both eventually buried. In 1845 navvies

Lewes Castle

discovered their remains while the railway line was being dug, and these were reinterred at the church of St John the Baptist in Southover High Street. The priory had long since been destroyed by Sir Thomas Cromwell at the Dissolution, but it is still ironic that the railway company should have been so cavalier with the ruins of a priory which, after all, was dedicated to St Pancras.

Barbican House at the entrance to the castle is the headquarters of the Sussex Archaeological Society. It contains a fine museum, and a record of all archaeological and historical work done within the county since the society was founded. The house was built in 1579 and purchased by the society in 1908.

Thomas Read Kemp who promoted Kemp Town in Brighton, was born at Barbican House in 1782.

Southover Grange was one of the buildings in Lewes built wholly or in part from stone removed from the priory. The grange was built in 1572 by an ancestor of Sir Isaac Newton, and John Evelyn the diarist was a boy there between 1630 and 1637. The very pleasant gardens possess a fine tulip tree.

The early sixteenth-century Anne of Cleves House in Southover High Street is another property of the Sussex Archaeological Society, used as a museum of Sussex life.

Bull House and the White Hart Hotel are associated with Tom Paine the pamphleteer and so-called 'Father of the

The Gatehouse, Lewes Castle

Lewes

PLACES OF INTEREST IN LEWES

Lewes Castle
Norman castle with shell keep and fourteenth-century barbican. Panoramic views of the Ouse valley.

Barbican House
Headquarters of the Sussex Archaeological Trust with a good museum of Sussex geology, geography and history.

Anne of Cleves House
Timber-framed house containing a Sussex folk museum and iron exhibits.

Southover Grange
Former home of diarist John Evelyn set in pretty gardens.

Military Heritage Museum
Displays of cavalry head-dress 1812-1914, and army history 1660-1914.

American Revolution'. He lived at Bull House from 1768 to 1774 while serving as an excise officer.

The burning of the Lewes Martyrs took place in 1557 when seventeen Protestants were executed for their faith by order of Queen Mary, who by this act alone earned the name 'Bloody Mary'. This event is commemorated by a memorial on Cliffe Hill and by Lewes Bonfire Boys every 5 November. It must be remembered by all who attend the bonfire celebrations in Lewes that it is not the present Pope who is burned in effigy, so offence should not be taken. Also the Lewes Bonfire Societies do not stage their events for the benefit of visitors, and would continue to hold them even if not an outsider attended. For those who do attend it is a memorable night, like nothing else in Britain.

Shelleys Hotel in the High Street was formerly The Vine. This is probably the oldest pub symbol in the world as the Romans used to hang a bunch of vine leaves outside their hostelries, and it is possible that this building occupies the site of one such. The present name is from the family of the poet.

St Michael's Church has one of the round towers unique to this area; the others are at Southease and Piddinghoe. No-one knows why the towers are round. It has been suggested that they also served as lighthouses, or that stone was not available for quoins.

The A275 which runs to Newhaven, passes through Southease and Piddinghoe, and also through Rodmell where for many years Virginia Woolf and her husband Leonard lived at Monks House, which they purchased in 1919. Tragically Virginia Woolf, who was subject to depression and worry, drowned herself in the Ouse in 1941. Rodmell has an old mulberry tree at South Farm. Many of the mulberry trees

Pevensey Roman Fort

Michelham Priory

The South Downs near Alfriston

Brighton seafront

to be found in Sussex date from around the beginning of the seventeenth century when James I made a determined effort to establish a silk industry, and the trees were planted so that silkworms could feed on the leaves.

Kiln Cottage in Piddinghoe (pronounced Piddnhoo) possesses the last survivor of a large brick making industry. This bottle-shaped brick kiln closed in about 1912. It was one of six which supplied bricks for several railway viaducts in Sussex. There is a pleasant but sad commemoration in the village known as 'Little Edith's Treat'. A baby named Edith Croft died in 1868, and her grandmother set up a fund of £100 so that her name be perpetuated with a church service, children's races, and a children's tea held every 19 July.

Piddinghoe people have long been the object of a number of Sussex jokes. It is variously said that they shoe magpies, hang their fields out to dry, fish for the moon, and dig for moonshine and smoke. However, these jokes are not intended to indicate the complete imbecility of local yokels; quite the reverse, for there is a simple explanation. The village was a centre for the manufacture of chalk whitening which was ground up in water and spread out to dry; the traditional Sussex oxen used for ploughing in the area were black and white and known as magpies, and needed to be shod, it was done in Piddinghoe; smugglers used to either bury their cargoes, or sink them in the river or in ponds, thus the alcohol (moonshine) and the tobacco (smoke) were recovered at night when locals 'fished for the moon'. It is said that a group of locals were discovered by excisemen one night busily fishing for cargo in the local pond. When asked what they were doing, quick as a flash they replied that they were trying to catch the large cheese that they had seen floating in the pond. The excisemen departed, laughing at the idiot yokels, but the villagers stayed, laughing at the credulous excisemen.

PLACES OF INTEREST AROUND LEWES

Bishopstone Church
Saxon church, humble and yet somehow grand.

Firle Place
Home of the Gage family for 500 years. Sèvres porcelain, English and French furniture, and pictures by Corregio, Guardi, Reynolds, Van Dyke, and Bartolommeo.

Glynde Place
Built in 1560, and containing fine needlework, rare bronzes, and pictures by Rubens, Zoffany, and Hofner.

Fort Newhaven
Napoleonic fort with gun emplacements; a maze of underground passages, and various exhibits.

Danny, Hurstpierpoint
'E' shaped house built in 1595. Fine great hall, paintings and ancient books.

Bentley Wildfowl, Halland
Over 1,000 birds of 110 species, and vintage cars. The house is good and the grounds are perfect for wandering.

Ditchling Common
188 acres of open countryside with nature trails and much wildlife.

Monks House, Rodmell (NT)
The home of Leonard and Virginia Woolf.

The Ouse has been a busy river since Roman times; iron trade barges were still regularly sailing up to Lewes at the beginning of this century.

North-east of Lewes the A26 heads towards Uckfield, of which E. V. Lucas again had something to say, 'It is agreeable to remember that Fanny Burney passed through the town with Mrs Thrale in 1779, although she found nothing to interest her.'

It was near Uckfield that one of the world's major scientific frauds took place when Charles Dawson amalgamated the skull of a man with the jawbone of an ape to produce Eanthropus Dawsoni, better known as Piltdown Man. When the discovery was made, the local inn changed its name from The Lamb to The Piltdown Man, and has not changed it back since.

Buxted is an iron town and it is here that Ralph Hogge or Huggett is reputed to have cast the first cannon. One of the Lewes Martyrs, Richard Woodman, came from Buxted, and the door in the church tower at Warbleton is attributed to him. There are several fine gardens in this area. Beeches Farm has both traditional and sunken gardens, Horsted Place has a charming Victorian garden, while Newick Park specialises in spring and autumn displays.

The triangle bounded by Brighton, Lewes, and Haywards Heath, contains Ditchling and Ditchling Beacon.

View from Ditchling Beacon

Ditchling has always had a reputation for attracting art and crafts people; Frank Brangwyn was a resident, and today Jill Pryke continues that tradition by creating extremely beautiful pottery and china. Ditchling Common is a nature reserve and Ditchling Beacon (813ft) is one of the finest viewpoints in the county. There are bell or disc barrows, disused dew-ponds, and at Clayton the famous windmills, Jack and Jill overlook it all. Jill is a smock mill built in 1821 at Dyke Road, Brighton, and was dragged bodily to her present abode by eighty-eight oxen in 1851. Jack, a tower mill, was built in 1866. Clayton railway tunnel entrance is battlemented like a piece of Arundel Castle with a small cottage perched incongruously amid the towers.

The lane near the tunnel leads to an E-shaped Elizabethan house, called Danny. It was built in 1593 and a wing was added in 1728, by Henry Campion. Lloyd George drew up the terms of the Armistice at Danny in 1918.

Burgess Hill is a railway town. Hilaire Belloc, visualising the day of judgement, foresaw that the world would perish in a rain of fire from heaven. Only Sussex would be saved, *notwithstanding* Burgess Hill. Hickstead is close at hand; the mecca of show-jumping, and appropriately once part of the manor of Saddlescombe.

Brighton is of course the major town in the Rape of Lewes and the largest town in Sussex, and is known as 'London by the sea', or the 'West End with winkles'. The town grew rapidly from small beginnings as a poor fishing village called Brighthelmstone, after Doctor Richard Russell published a tract entitled *A Dissertation Concerning the Use of Sea Water in Diseases of the Glands* and commenced his treatments which involved immersing the exterior and the interior of the unfortunate patient in seawater. By the time he died (he was buried in his native Lewes in 1759) the fortunes of Brighton were in the ascendant. The arrival of the Prince

The beach, Brighton

Regent to live with his mistress in 1783 set the seal on Brighton's successful development.

Mrs Fitzherbert was soon translated secretly from mistress to wife, but continued to live at Steyne House, now the YMCA. In the meantime the Prince Regent had acquired a small house around the corner which he set Henry Holland to enlarge in 1785. In 1822 he engaged Nash to do further work, and the Royal Pavilion, that eastern fantasy, was born.

Most people either love it or hate it. The Rev Sidney Smith said that it looked as if St Pauls had come to the seaside and pupped! Cobbett made remarks about turnips on boxes, and Queen Victoria was not amused. It was acquired by the town in 1850 for £50. The dome was originally the stable block and was built in 1803-8, and the North Gate was built in 1832 to commemorate William IV. The Pavilion has been and still is being tastefully restored, and is an experience not to be missed. The furniture, the decor, the marvellous chandeliers, and the wonderful kitchens, are all slightly larger than life, leaving an abiding impression of colour and gaiety.

By the early decades of the nineteenth century wholesale development was taking place in Brighton, and many of the famous terraces date from this period. Sussex Square, Kemp Town was designed by C. A. Busby in 1824, Royal Crescent was built by 1807 and Decimus Burton completed Adelaide Crescent by 1850.

During the later part of the nineteenth century more of the now familiar landmarks were erected: the West Pier in 1886 and the Palace Pier in 1899. Magnus Volk opened the first electric public railway in 1883, still running today, and the Aquarium opened in 1872. The Aquarium is now also a Dolphinarium where the skills of these mysterious creatures are demonstrated every day.

The parish church of St Nicholas is a survivor from old Brighthelmstone, dating from the fourteenth century. The churchyard contains several memorials to people famous in Brighton and far beyond. One of these is Captain Tettersall who spirited Charles II across to France and later, after the restoration of 'Old Rowley' to the throne, sailed up the Thames with his boat dressed throughout to claim his reward.

Martha Gunn, one of the original 'dippers' or women bathing attendants, and by all accounts a tough old biddy, is also buried here, as is Phoebe Hessell who enlisted in the army as a man, fought in the 5th Regiment of Foot and was wounded at Fontenoy. She did it for love, to be with her man when he enlisted. She eventually married her man and lived to be 108. No-one knows how she kept her identity secret during her seventeen years of military service, but certainly it must have taken formidable mental discipline.

The railway came to Brighton in 1841, and greatly changed the pattern of development by bringing a different

---

PLACES OF INTEREST IN AND AROUND UCKFIELD

Beeches Farm, Uckfield
Attractive garden with lawns, yew trees, borders, sunken garden, and roses.

Bridge Cottage, Uckfield
A timber-framed fourteenth-century wealden house.

Horsted Place Gardens, Uckfield
House of Lord Nevill. The charming Victorian garden contains rhododendrons, rose borders, and shaded walks.

Newick Park
A fine garden featuring azaleas, rhododendrons, Italian gardens, plus bluebells, primulas, daffodils, and roses. There is also a farmland walk.

kind of holidaymaker, but this trend had been started by the stage-coach. Cobbett was able to write in 1823; 'Brighton is so situated that a coach, which leaves at not very early in the morning, reached London by noon: and starting to go back in two hours and a half afterwards reached Brighton not very late at night. Great parcels of stockjobbers stay at Brighton with the women and children. They skip backwards and forward on the coaches and actually carry on

Interior of the Royal Pavilion, Brighton

stockjobbing in Change Alley though they reside in Brighton.' So began the city gent commuting up to town.

The stage-coach run to Brighton became so efficient that for a few years the resort became the main cross-channel port. The railway finished Brighton as a cross-channel port, but it opened up a new trade which has lasted until today. In 1844 the first excursion train left London Bridge bound for Brighton with two thousand passengers aboard. When they arrived they had whelks. So the Brighton of the Prince Regent became the Brighton of Mr Smith.

But Brighton never lost its racy image, and a weekend there still has vastly different connotations to a weekend at Budleigh Salterton; or indeed Hove which plays Jekyll to Brighton's Hyde. Graham Greene in *Brighton Rock* portrayed a Brighton of race gangs and touts, but Brighton Races, begun in 1783, offer racing and scenery as good as anywhere except perhaps Goodwood.

Although no longer a port, Brighton has developed a massive marina where yachts and small craft of all kinds jostle together in what old salts would have called a gallimaufry. HMS *Cavalier*, the last surviving World War II destroyer rests here guarding its last convoy. The road leading to the marina, Madeira Drive, is the destination for the London to Brighton Veteran Car Run, as well as the scene for other vintage vehicle events and speed trials.

Dyke Road leads to Devils Dyke and also to the Booth Museum of Natural History, with a beautiful display of over five hundred birds in their natural habitats, butterflies, and a section on conservation. Devils Dyke, a well known beauty spot, is a rift in the Downs supposedly made by the Devil enraged at the sight of so many churches in Sussex. While navvying away one night to let the sea in to drown the offending churches, the Devil was

---

PLACES OF INTEREST IN BRIGHTON

British Engineerium
A huge collection covering engineering history, including hundreds of full-size and model engines, tools, fire and steam engines, and a beam water pump.

Dolphinarium and Aquarium
Dolphin shows, sealions, seals, marine, tropical and freshwater fish.

Preston Manor
Old manor house with a fine collection of furniture, glass, silver and china.

Royal Pavilion
The unique mogul place of the Prince Regent, containing some of the most superb interiors in the world. Fantastic Regency Chinese decor.

Booth Museum, Dyke Road
Displays of over 500 cases of British birds in their natural surroundings plus skeletons, and a huge collection of butterflies.

HMS Cavalier, The Marina
The only surviving destroyer to have served in World War II, moored in the largest marina in Europe.

Volks Railway
Britain's first public electric railway, opened in 1883.

Palace Pier
Built in 1899 and containing the National Museum of Slot Machines.

The Lanes
Brighton's old town, world famous for its antique shops, and its atmosphere.

disturbed by an old woman holding a candle behind a seive and prodding a cock until it crowed. Thinking it was morning the Devil fled and never returned to try again.

Preston Manor is not far away. This old manor house was built about 1250, and rebuilt in 1738 by Thomas Western. It was presented to Brighton by Sir Charles Thomas-Stanford in 1932, and the rooms are kept as they were in the owner's lifetime, with period furniture, silver, glass, and china. The Anne of Cleves room has walls covered with leather squares brought to England by Catherine of Aragon.

Hove is always described as genteel, and perhaps the time has come when this should be considered a positive virtue. There is, after all, nothing wrong with wanting parks and gardens, and civilised neighbours. Furthermore, Hove is the home of Sussex cricket, and a place which has provided the world with the talents of C. B. Fry, Maurice Tate, the Coxes, the Langridges, the Parks, and Ted Dexter, must rate as a shrine to all true cricket lovers. Hove is also the home of the British Engineerium, a living steam museum. As well as two compound engines, there are numerous models, full size engines, tools, and other exhibits.

West Blatchington, just north of Hove, has a windmill that perches on a barn. It is the oldest existing smock mill in Sussex, dating from 1724, and reputedly its sails were used to signal to smugglers.

Further north still, the pretty village of Henfield is the headquarters of the Sussex Trust for Nature Conservation at Woods Mill. This is a watermill with a nature trail. Inside the mill the trust have arranged some very imaginative exhibitions covering the wildlife in the area, and the life in their own ponds. Incidentally, be sure to notice The Cat House covered with wrought iron cats.

The remaining part of the Lewes Rape is the stretch of cliffs starting at Black Rock in Brighton and ending at

The Lanes, Brighton

Newhaven. The A259 passes Roedean School on its way to Rottingdean, where Kipling lived before removing to Burwash. The house called The Elms is where he wrote his poem 'If'.

The windmill at Rottingdean is possibly the most famous in the world as it is used as the logo for Heinemanns the publishers. Built in 1802, it was saved from destruction by an appeal launched by Hilaire Belloc in 1922. Standing right on the cliffs this windmill was also the subject of unkind rumours regarding the setting of the sails, the position of the excise patrols, and the landing of cargoes.

Rottingdean has some fine timber framed houses tucked away from the main road, including a small Tudor

West Blatchington Windmill

PLACES OF INTEREST AROUND
BRIGHTON

Bramber Castle
Gaunt remains of the castle of de
Braose as left by Cromwell.

House of Pipes, Bramber
A museum of smokers and smoking
through the ages with nearly 50,000
exhibits.

Woods Mill, Henfield
Headquarters of the Sussex Trust for
Nature Conservation with a
watermill, interesting displays, and
nature trails.

Rottingdean Windmill
A smock mill which was the model
for the Heinemann logo.

Clayton Mills, Ditchling
A tower mill, Jack, and a smock mill,
Jill, standing near Ditchling Beacon.
Jill was dragged to her site bodily on
skis.

Oldland Mill, Keymer
An ancient post mill dating from
about 1690.

West Blatchington Mill
The oldest smock mill in Sussex,
standing on a barn.

Devil's Dyke
A well known beauty spot formed by
a cleft in the South Downs, allegedly
carved by Old Nick himself.

Sompting Church
Saxon church with a unique 'Rhenish
Helm' roof, dating from around
AD960.

courtyard with small houses all facing
inwards, of absolutely breathtaking
perfection. Much of Rottingdean was
destroyed in 1377 during several French
raids on various parts of the coast, and
the rebuilding ensured that many of its
houses date from that period, as is the
case with Rye, destroyed in the same
year. The Grange Museum houses part
of the National Toy Museum with many
fascinating clockwork wonders. There is
also a room dedicated to Kipling.

There is not much that can be said
about Peacehaven, which was a 'homes
for heroes' development for ex-
servicemen after World War I. The
Greenwich Meridian passes through
Peacehaven, and who can blame it.
North of Peacehaven lies Telscombe, a
village that makes Peacehaven even
more incomprehensible.

The South Downs near Edburton

4 Inland Sussex (East)

Ticehurst is a pleasant little village of mainly weatherboarded cottages standing on a high ridge. It was the first place in England to grow flax, although it was also surrounded by deposits of iron. The church of St Mary has a good brass to John Wybarne (1490), and a magnificent font canopy of the fifteenth century with flamboyant tracery and a folding door. The room (parvise) over the north porch has a strong oaken door suitable for its former use as a prison. A member of the greatly dreaded Hawkhurst smuggling gang lived just

outside Ticehurst at a place known as Seacox Heath; George Gray often used the Bell Inn which is said to date from the fifteenth century.

There is an iron grave-slab in the church at Ticehurst, but Wadhurst can boast thirty, dating between 1617 and 1790. They are all bedded in the church floor, and look very handsome. Many of them mark the burials of members of the Barham family; they were iron-masters, who claimed descent from Robert de Berham, a son of Reginald Fitzurse, one of Becket's murderers.

Iron grave slabs in Wadhurst church

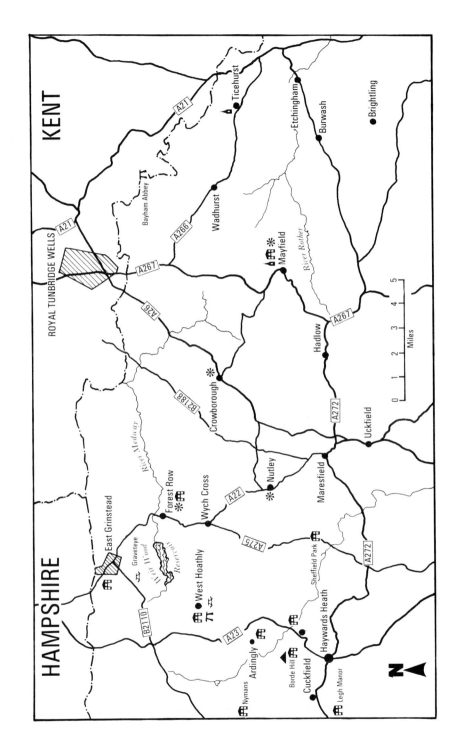

Oast-houses near Wadhurst

Iron has been mined in this area since Roman times and by 1253 Wadhurst had received its charter. The main street today is an attractive mixture of houses ranging from Tudor to Georgian. The huge reservoir at Bewl Bridge, begun in 1976, now offers such attractions as aquatic sports, bird-watching, and

Bewl Bridge Reservoir host many activities and events

Bewl Bridge

nature trails; at advertised times events such as craft fairs are staged here too.

Frant parish contains the remains of Bayham Abbey, just off the B2169 road from Lamberhurst to Tunbridge Wells. The abbey was Premonstratensian after the parent house at Prémontré, near Laon in north-eastern France. The house followed a rule of life ascribed to St Augustine of Hippo. Bayham Abbey was built between 1200 and 1234 and was soon involved in a prolonged quarrel with Michelham Priory over the ownership of Hailsham church, which Bayham eventually won.

Hartfield

Mayfield

Bayham was dissolved in 1525 and given to Sir Anthony Browne (who also collected Battle Abbey and Cowdray Park). The ruins are very romantic and remind one of Fountains Abbey in Yorkshire. It was landscaped by Humphrey Repton in 1800 to enhance the romantic effect.

Shernfold Park at Frant was the home of one Colonel By who founded Bytown in Canada. It is now famous as Ottawa.

Mayfield seems to have been a venue for regular contests between the Devil and St Dunstan, who had a forge in the village. It is said that the Devil came to tempt the saint in the guise of a beautiful girl but was careless enough to allow a cloven hoof to be seen, whereupon St Dunstan seized the nose of the Devil with his red-hot tongs. Old Nick roared and with one bound reached Tunbridge Wells where he plunged his nose into a spring, thus giving the water the taste which it has retained ever since. On another occasion St Dunstan thwarted

the Devil's plan to knock down the village by nailing a horseshoe on every door. Of course, coming from Glastonbury, reputed to be the holiest spot in Britain, St Dunstan was well qualified to deal with Satan; and was Archbishop of Canterbury from 960 to 988. Mayfield Palace was used by the archbishops for 250 years, and many nobles and ecclesiastics visited this favourite summer residence. Edward I paid three visits, and Queen Elizabeth one. The last Archbishop to use the palace was Cranmer who gave it to Henry VIII.

Other grand old buildings include the Middle House Hotel (1575), Yeomans (1420), Walnut Tree House (about 1450), Aylwins, and the Old Brewhouse. Coventry Patmore praised this village with good cause, representing as it does all that is best in the weald.

The post mill which stands at the junction of the A267 and the B2101 is Argos Hill Mill. It was built sometime between 1831 and 1843 and worked until 1927. It has a traditional Sussex fantail assembly and is in very good condition following restoration in the 1960s. It is hoped that it will once again open to the public if a voluntary body can be formed to provide staff.

The church of St Dunstan is a replacement for one destroyed by fire in 1389, and is mainly in the Perpendicular style. It has a squat, shingled broach spire similar to the spire at Mountfield. It is said that the first church on this site was a wooden one built by St Dunstan in 960, which he and the Devil pushed sideways and then straight for a while before the Devil gave up the unequal struggle.

Mayfield Village sign is a famous attraction; it shows children dancing in a grassy meadow, as the village name means virgins' or maids' field.

Rotherfield is where the eastern Rother rises to start its journey to Rye. At one time the river ran to New Romney but the great storm in 1287, when 'the sea flowed twice without ebbing', totally changed its course. The source of the Medway and one of the sources of the Ouse are also in this area. The church is dedicated to St Denys because Berhtwald, a South Saxon Duke, made a pilgrimage to the monastery of St Denis when 'incurably' ill and made a miraculous recovery. In his gratitude he founded the church in 792. It has a slender shingled spire which is a landmark for miles around. Although a beautiful church, the inside strikes the visitor as being slightly austere despite the raked box pews, the Laudian pulpit with a sounding board, a wagon roof and medieval wall paintings.

Rotherfield has a number of tile-hung,

Mayfield

Sheffield Park Gardens

---

or weather-boarded, cottages and an inn, the King's Arms, said to be haunted by the ghost of Maurice Tate, the Sussex and England bowler who was once landlord. Rotherfield Hall and Old Manor are two other notable buildings.

A strange legend has grown up about the women of Rotherfield. It is said that they are unusually tall, although how this is achieved is a matter of some controversy. Some say that Rotherfield women have an extra pair of ribs, while others insist that in fact it is not their bodies but their legs which are elongated through constantly having to be pulled out of clinging clay.

Crowborough is a not particularly attractive town, although there is a magnificent view across the Ashdown Forest from The Beacon, which rises to 800ft. Sir Henry Fermor, a Sussex ironmaster who died in 1734, regarded the people of Crowborough with a somewhat jaundiced eye. He left money

in trust to build a charity school 'for the use and benefit of the very ignorant and heathenish people of Crowborough'.

Richard Jefferies and Sir Arthur Conan Doyle both lived here, as did J. M. Barrie. Possibly it was the attraction of the Ashdown Forest that brought them to the area. It was once a Royal Forest and the king hunted there amid trees of all kinds, but the tree-felling associated with the iron industry left the heathland which exists today. In prehistoric times great lizards roamed, and at the time of Domesday there was pannage for 34,000 hogs. There were even wolves and wild boar. The Romans called it *Sylva Anderida* and started extracting iron ore; the Saxons called it *Andreaswald* and developed agriculture. William Cobbett was less than enthusiastic: '. . . Ashurst [sic] Forest, which is a heath, with here and there a few birch scrubs upon it, verily the most villainously ugly spot I ever saw in

England. This lasts you for five miles, getting, if possible, uglier and uglier all the way, till at last, as if barren soil, nasty spewy gravel, heath and even that stunted, were not enough, you see rising spot, which instead of trees, presents you with black, ragged, hideous rocks. . . .' Of course he was much nearer in time to the devastation that the iron industry created, which caused the Tudors to fear that there would be no trees left for building ships, thus rendering the new-fangled cast cannon much less useful. Sailors on the other hand were complaining that their ordnance was inferior to that of their enemies. Although sometimes true, it was often the case that they were being fired upon by English guns smuggled into Europe. The problem of balancing iron with

Sheffield Park House

The Bluebell Line

timber was ultimately solved by the shortage of timber in the south and the use of coal to smelt iron in the north. The iron industry in this area suffered a rapid decline and nature set about repairing the ravaged forest. Today the bracken and the heather grow on beautiful heathland where nightingales sing, and that strange bird, the nightjar, makes its home.

Hartfield was of course the home of A. A. Milne, Christopher Robin, and Winnie-The-Pooh. Poohsticks Bridge is still there, and so is Cotchford Farm where it was all written. Wych Cross has a complete gun-casting pit, plus two recently excavated furnaces. It also has a good example of the unusual milestones which bear a bow and three bells and the mileage to London, that are found in some parts of the Weald.

Simon de Montfort made camp at Fletching before the Battle of Lewes in 1264, and Edward Gibbon the historian is buried at the church. The name almost certainly means that it was a centre for

making arrows, a trade which flourished in wartime and also provided for hunting, official and otherwise. 'The people of Fletching live by snapping and ketching' is an old Sussex saying, referring to poaching as much as anything else. The church of St Mary and St Andrew contains a fine canopied brass to Sir Edward Dalyngrigge and his wife, and an unusual little brass of a pair of gloves, commemorating Peter Denot who supported Jack Cade and who was a glover by trade.

Sheffield Park is now chiefly known for its gardens, kept in superb condition by the National Trust. The Australians used to play the first match of their cricket tours here, before Arundel Park became the venue. The famous gardens were laid out for John Baker Holroyd, first Earl of Sheffield, between 1769 and 1794 by Capability Brown and Humphrey Repton. The trees and shrubs were introduced by Arthur Soames who bought the estate in 1910. The ornamental lakes are a particular feature of the garden, probably in part having originally been hammer ponds. The house is partly Tudor but was rebuilt and enlarged by James Wyatt in 1775. Edward Gibbon wrote part of *The Decline and Fall of the Roman Empire* while living there as a guest of the first earl.

Just along the road, the Bluebell Line runs from Sheffield Park to Horsted Keynes. Laid down in 1882 this is the only remaining section of the Lewes to East Grinstead line run by the London, Brighton and South Coast Railway. Closed in 1959, it was reopened as a private line in 1960. The locomotive stock is normally around thirty-five engines which include a West Country class, *Blackmore Vale*, a Schools class, *Stowe*, and *Stepney* immortalised in the stories of the Rev Awdry. The sheds are an absolute delight and the whole enterprise is one of the finest preserved railways in Britain. The line is a living museum of steam and the Southern Railway, and brightens a dull day and a drab age.

Nutley has the oldest working windmill in Sussex. It is a lovely old mill, built around 1675 at Crowborough (although some say it came from Goudhurst in Kent) and moved to the present site in 1810. As well as being the oldest working windmill in Sussex, it is also the smallest. It is unusual in that it is a post mill of the open-trestle type, with no roundhouse. It has no fantail and was pushed into the wind with a tail pole. Nutley mill ceased working commercially in 1908 and after extensive restoration by the Uckfield and District Preservation Society the sails turned again in 1971 to drive two pairs of stones.

Ardingly also provides a treat for steam lovers. Once a year, about a fortnight after the South of England Show, Ardingly showground is filled with traction engines, showmen's engines, steamrollers, vintage vehicles, several sideshows and fairground organs and a fun fair. It always makes a

wonderful day out, and nearly always seems to attract good weather. The South of England Show is also worth attending, as it is one of the best agricultural shows in England.

Ardingly Reservoir offers canoeing, sailing, trout fishing, nature trails, picnic areas, and scenery of a very high order. Weir Wood Reservoir near Forest Row also offers fishing and bird watching, and as with all the Southern Water Authority reservoirs (including Ardingly) it is well run and looked after. The area around Ardingly could well be dubbed garden country, for three of the great gardens of the south-east are within easy reach. Wakehurst Place 'Kew Gardens in the country', is an important collection of exotic trees, shrubs, and other plants, with a picturesque watercourse linking several lakes and ponds. There is in addition a heath garden and rock walk, and a natural history exhibition in the mansion, which was built in 1590 by Sir Edward Culpeper.

Borde Hill Garden is large, with woods and parkland where there are many rare and exotic trees and shrubs, as well as a full range of camellias, rhododendrons, magnolias, and azaleas. There is a Judas tree, a Chinese tulip tree, a handkerchief tree and many rarities from China and the Himalayas. The statue of a veiled lady on the West Terrace is called 'The Bride' and is by Antonio Tantardini of Milan.

Nymans Garden at Handcross also contains most of the plants mentioned above. Rhododendrons do particularly well in the weald, and in some places they are coming to be regarded as weeds. The large, walled, romantic garden, the sunken garden, and the laurel walk, all centred around the romantic ruins of the house, make this one of the great gardens of the South East.

Cuckfield used to be a market town, holding a charter from Henry III and another from Charles II. It was on the coaching route from London to Brighton. Three days every week the

Lindfield

---

strangely named 'Brighthelmstone and Cuckfield Machine' left London at 5am. That was in 1780; by 1828 fifty coaches were passing through every day. It is not generally realised how great the coaching trade was. Every town of any consequence had at least one inn, often with stables and change-horses. Fifty pairs of horses were kept at Cuckfield alone, and over 800 coaches a day passed through Marble Arch. The coming of the railways changed all this within a few decades, causing considerable distress and unemployment. Stable hands, inn staff, harness-makers, coach builders, feed suppliers, tanners, and smithies lost their livelihood. Previously important inns suddenly became deserted; many, occupying previously vital positions at crossroads, or deep in the country, lost their trade almost overnight, often becoming completely isolated. It is possible that the high level of smuggling at this time was due in part to the

unemployment of both men and horses, and the large number of inns suddenly in quiet places with plenty of storage space and stabling.

Cuckfield was the home of the Sergison family who, according to Augustine Hare, established in Haywards Heath 'a colony of cockney villas' by selling off the land in small parcels. Like most developers, they lived in a beautiful house isolated from their creations. Their house, Legh Manor at Ansty, just south of Cuckfield, was built between 1530 and 1550, and another portion was added by Sir Edwin Lutyens in a very similar manner to his work at Great Dixter, even to the extent of planning the garden with the advice of Gertrude Jekyll.

The garden at Heaselands has been created solely by its owner, Ernest Kleinwort. It spreads across a wide shallow valley and the small stream running through it has been dammed at several points to create a continuous river-like lake. Many migrating water fowl use this lake and add to its attraction. Near the house there are lawns and flower beds flanked by trees and shrubs, but further away there is an extensive woodland garden with rhododendrons and azaleas, the whole garden comprising some thirty acres.

All the main railway lines into Sussex were completed by the 1850s and Haywards Heath is one of the towns that developed as a result, mainly because Cuckfield did not want the railway. The consequence is that Haywards Heath has outgrown Cuckfield.

Lindfield is a picture postcard village. The main street is long and lined with pleasing houses, with the mainly thirteenth-century church at one end, and a large pond at the other. Adwulf, Duke of the South Saxons, gave lands in Lindfield to endow the monastery of Malling. There was a weekly market and two annual fairs in the fourteenth century. The church was ruthlessly restored in 1884, with an unbelievably crass destruction of medieval glass and painting. Just behind the church is a fine Elizabethan house called Old Place; and about a mile east is another, East Mascalls. East Mascalls has been called 'one of the most beautiful of timbered houses in Sussex, or indeed in England'.

Heading back towards Crawley and East Grinstead the road passes Worth, which has the only Saxon cruciform church in Britain which is complete and untouched in plan. There are no aisles or central tower. The tower at the north end is of much later date. The quoins exhibit typical long and short work of the Saxon period. The chief beauty of the church is the chancel arch; 22ft high and the finest and largest Saxon arch in Britain. The arches of the transepts are similar but smaller. There are three Saxon two-light windows high up in the nave, and there is a 'Devil's Door' in the north wall. The carved wooden pulpit is from Germany, and the carved oak rails are probably of a similar origin and date (1541). The lych-gate is sixteenth century and a good one with an impressive stone roof. Worth church, dedicated to St Nicholas, was probably built late in the tenth century or early in the eleventh. It certainly pre-dates the conquest by a considerable margin although oddly, it is not mentioned in Domesday Book.

The Priest's House at West Hoathly is a folk museum housed in an early fifteenth century house with a very attractive Horsham slab roof, and a cottage garden.

At this point it might be appropriate to draw attention to a feature of Sussex which can cause considerable confusion. Places which sound as if they belong together are frequently far apart. East Hoathly, for example, is near Hailsham. East Chiltington is near Lewes, whereas West Chiltington is near Storrington. Upper Beeding is on low land near Bramber; Lower Beeding is on high ground above Cowfold. West Blatchington is a suburb of Brighton; East Blatchington is a suburb of Seaford, while Upwaltham and Coldwaltham are about ten miles apart by road, and Upper Hartfield is below Hartfield. That also applies to the Dickers: Upper is below Lower. Then there are Saddlescombe and Sedlescombe; Easebourne and Eastbourne; Ifield and Isfield; Bognor and Bignor; and Handcross and Cross-in-Hand!

Before leaving West Hoathly completely, those who are interested in industrial bygones may be interested to visit Tanyard at Sharpthorne, an interesting small museum devoted to leather preparation and tanning.

Standen was built between 1892 and 1894. It is a large family house designed by Philip Webb, a friend of William Morris. The remarkably complete interior has been carefully restored, including the William Morris wallpaper and textiles. There is also a hillside garden with very fine views.

East Grinstead tends to give the impression that it belongs in Surrey. The most notable building is Sackville

College, founded by Robert, Earl of Dorset in 1608. The quadrangle is a fine example of the Jacobean style and the fireplace and furniture in the main hall are good. John Mason Neale, the hymn writer, was once warden of this college; he wrote 'Good King Wenceslas', and 'Jerusalem the Golden'.

Sackville College was originally established to house twenty-one men and ten women (unmarried) from among the earl's pensioned servants, and the prayer of the inmates since 1619 includes the line 'I pray God bless my Lord of Dorset and my ladie, and all their posteritie'.

As one would expect with a town containing Sackville College and the old Judge's House used during the Assizes, East Grinstead is far older than it appears. It returned two Members of Parliament for five hundred years until 1832, and still retains one. Quite a number of the shops in the High Street are re-fronted timber-framed buildings, here and there with roofs slabbed with Horsham stone. Three citizens of the town were burned during the Marian persecutions in 1556; not surprisingly Sussex almost completely sided with the Parliamentary forces a hundred years later. Iron has been worked in this area since Roman times — the nearby Roman road at Holtye is estimated to have contained 35,000 tons of slag and cinders. The Domesday Book records an iron mine at East Grinstead, and in 1266 Henry III made a grant of a penny on each load conveyed to Lewes.

The church of St Swithun has a lofty

PLACES OF INTEREST IN AND AROUND EAST GRINSTEAD

Sackville College, East Grinstead
Jacobean almshouse with fine antique oak furniture.

Argos Windmill, Mayfield
Post mill from about 1831 with traditional Sussex fantail assembly.

Ashdown Forest
6,500 acres of heathland and woods for walking and picnics.

Barnsgate Manor, near Uckfield
21-acre vineyard offering tours and tastings, plus a wine museum.

Cobblers Garden, Crowborough
A water garden, rare shrubs, and herbacious borders.

Sheffield Park (NT)
Magnificent eighteenth-century garden by Capability Brown with beautiful lakes. Autumn tints are superb. The house (not NT) is partly Tudor, rebuilt in the eighteenth century.

Borde Hill, Haywards Heath
Over 300 acres of gardens and woodlands, with rose trees, camellias and rhododendrons.

Kidbrooke Park, Forest Row
Parkland with a wild garden, a bog garden, a pergola, and a ha-ha.

Forest Way Nature Trail
Linear park following route of old railway from East Grinstead to Groombridge.

Nutley Windmill
The oldest, and smallest, working post mill in Sussex. Open-trestle type built in 1675.

Standen, East Grinstead (NT)
A hillside garden offering wonderful views over Ashdown Forest.

Spring Hill Wildfowl Park, Forest Row
Over 1,000 birds including rare species in a beautiful 10-acre park.

tower which can be seen from some distance, but it is a replacement for the original which fell down in 1785, damaging the church quite badly. It was rebuilt by James Wyatt, but the work, which started in 1789, was not completed until 1813. It could be that this was due to financial problems, because a rhyme from that period states:
    'Large parish, poor people;
    Large new church, no steeple.'
The interior is Georgian gothic and a good example of its type.

The wildfowl park at Forest Row, Spring Hill, has a collection of almost a thousand birds, a number of them extremely rare. It is off the A22, and by one of those little coincidences which fit so well, the turning is by the Swan Hotel. The birds potter around in the ten acre grounds; rheas with cranes, flamingos with rare geese.

Forest Row has another beautiful garden in an area of beautiful gardens. Kidbrooke Park dates from the early eighteenth century, when Lord William Neville built the mansion and created a park out of forest and heath. The parkland was laid out by Humphrey Repton with a wild garden, a bog garden, a walled garden, a pergola, and a 'ha-ha' (a sunken ditch with a retaining wall).

A new interpretation centre and centre for the forest rangers has been opened at Wych Cross. Three ancient barns were dismantled and painstakingly re-erected at the new site to make a very attractive and useful amenity.

Chelwood Gate is the home of Lord Stockton, better known as Sir Harold Macmillan; another famous Chelwood Gate resident was Viscount Cecil, founder of the Leage of Nations.

5 From Shoreham to Arundel

When carrying out his policy of placing each rape in the care of a trusted henchman, William the Conqueror selected for the Rape of Bramber which covers this area, William de Braose. This knight, when endeavouring to subdue Gwent, invited the Welsh chiefs to a banquet and parley at Abergavenny, and then murdered them. The Conqueror made de Braose his chancellor; and he built the castle at Bramber between 1070 and 1073. Cromwell's troops knocked it down in 1644, after a siege, leaving only the gaunt ruins on their mound, which are there today.

When the castle was built, the sea ran up an inlet to Steyning, which was then a port, and Bramber Castle once guarded passage from the sea; the waters then coming close to the castle mound. The Saxon name for Bramber was *Brymmburh,* a fortified hill, so it seems likely that there was a previous fort on the present site.

De Braose, with that mixture of piety and brutality found in many of the Normans, also built the church of St Nicholas as a chapel for the castle, built another church in Shoreham, and made a pilgrimage to the Holy Land. He built a great bridge as well and imposed tariffs on passing boats, with his officers and boat crews frequently having pitched battles in the streets.

The St Nicholas to whom a number of Sussex churches are dedicated, including the one above, is of course Santa Claus; however, dedications of churches are made due to the fact that he is patron saint of seafarers, rather than children. St Nicholas once saved three girls from slavery by casting three golden balls through their father's open window for their dowries. This came to form the basis of the saint's symbol, and was adopted by pawnbrokers; it is also the basis of the legend of Santa Claus bringing presents at night.

William de Braose never returned from his pilgrimage, and his son Philip took part in the first crusade. This led to the establishment in the area of the Order of the Temple of Solomon in Jerusalem, an order of fighting monks better known as Knights Templars. Part of Bramber was donated to the order by Philip's widow. The Templars were also granted the church at Sompting, and owned The Chapel House, part of which is now incorporated into the lovely house St Mary's. The great bridge, with the chapel of St Mary in the centre, stood approximately where the car park of St Mary's is sited.

In 1312, the Templars were ruthlessly suppressed on charges of unlawful arts and gross immorality, although more probably because of their immense power. Bramber passed to the Priory of Sele, which had been founded by William de Braose in 1080 as a branch of the Benedictine monastery of St Florent at Saumur in Anjou. The town prospered under this order for two hundred years, until a further charge of gross immorality was made, and the priory was dissolved in 1539. The history of this, and other priories in Sussex, would explain why Monk, Abbot, Parsons and Prior are comparatively common surnames in the county!

Charles II sheltered at St Mary's before his escape from Shoreham, and there were one or two minor skirmishes during the Civil War. Bramber then became a 'rotten borough', and the immorality became temporal. William Wilberforce once stopped in Bramber to ask where he was. Upon being informed, he exclaimed, 'Why, this must be the

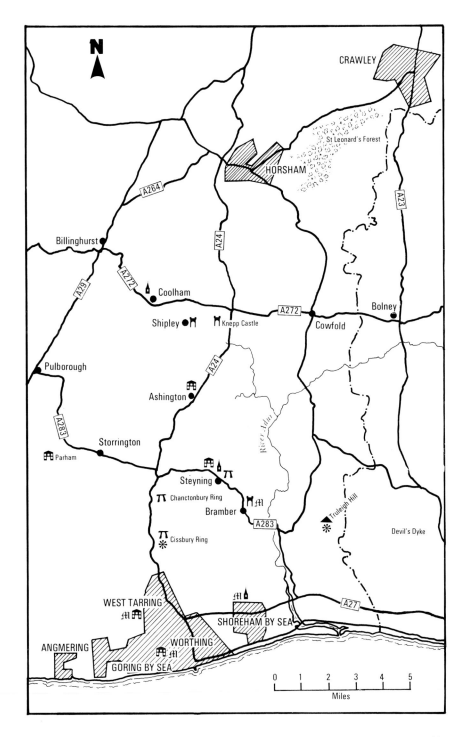

CRAWLEY

St Leonard's Forest

HORSHAM

A264

A24

A23

Billinghurst

A29

A272

Coolham

Shipley

Knepp Castle

A272

Bolney

Cowfold

Pulborough

A24

A283

Ashington

River Adur

Storrington

Parham

Steyning

Chanctonbury Ring

Bramber

A283

Truleigh Hill

Devil's Dyke

Cissbury Ring

A27

WEST TARRING

SHOREHAM BY SEA

ANGMERING

WORTHING

GORING BY SEA

0   1   2   3   4   5
Miles

place I'm Member for.' Nicholas Barbon, the originator of fire insurance, was a member also. When the Reform Act of 1832 ended this state of affairs, Bramber was described as the 'most rotten' of the rotten boroughs, with eighteen voters and two MPs!

Bramber was at one time the site of the Potter Museum of Curiosities, which is now at Arundel. Its place was taken by a 'smokiana'. This collection of some 50,000 exhibits of anything to do with smoking, covers more than 250 countries and 1500 years.

Steyning was a flourishing town before the Romans came, and the Romans settled extensively in the area. By the time of Alfred and Great it was a royal possession, and his father Ethelwulf was buried in Steyning in 858.

The church of St Andrew is worthy of more detailed mention. It is basically a late Norman building, erected by the monks of Fécamp, who were given the site by Edward the Confessor in 1047. The grave slab in the porch has been variously ascribed to St Cuthman, Ethelwulf, and also to the Celts, with the crosses added later. The early church was probably cruciform, and larger than the present building, as the foundations of a choir larger than the present chancel have been discovered. The more crudely carved arches at the east end of the aisles, the aisle walls, and a window on the north side are early Norman. The chancel arch, nave arcades and clerestory, are late Norman or early Transitional. There are rich mouldings of the scallop, chevron, cable, fern, palm-leaf, saw-tooth, and Sarcenic honeycomb types, and the font is late Norman. The tower is sixteenth century, and the aisle windows are Perpendicular.

Around the middle of the fourteenth century, the sea began to recede from Steyning and the river became a stream. The harbour of Steyning became

Bramber Castle

completely inaccessible to shipping, and no longer commercially useful. Steyning turned its attention inland, and became instead a market town, entitled to hold a market twice a week and a fair twice a year.

At the junction of High Street and Church Street stands the Grammar School, founded in 1614. There are other buildings to delight camera enthusiasts, or those who prefer wandering and looking. Saxon Cottage, Chequers Yard, and Chanctonbury Cottage are all worth finding. The Old Market House once staged a meeting for George Fox, founder of the Quakers, and in Horsham Road stands Penns House where William Penn preached in 1670.

Steyning is overlooked by what is certainly the most famous landmark in Sussex; Chanctonbury Ring. The ring is an earthwork round which Charles Goring of Wiston planted beech trees in 1760. Some of the trees are now looking rather weary, and some rather unsuitable trees have been planted, but from a distance the ring is unmistakable. A Roman temple was discovered there, and it has, perhaps, always been a sacred spot, if ability to generate superstition and folklore is any measure. Examples of legends are that you can raise Julius Caesar and his army by counting the trees, and you can raise the devil if you run seven times around them. However, you will not be tempted to run around anything once you have reached the summit, as the path to it is, in places, extremely steep. Once there though, you can see most of Sussex, and parts of Hampshire and Surrey; the view is stunningly beautiful.

There are two other fine viewpoints within easy reach of Steyning, and both are important prehistoric sites. Truleigh Hill has linchets, terrace ways, and a Celtic road.

Cissbury is the largest of all the earthworks in Sussex, probably dating from about 280BC, and covering nearly eighty acres, with ramparts stretching for more than a mile. Within this fortified city there are Neolithic flint mines which were as important as Grimes Graves in Norfolk. Cissbury has been compared, justifiably, with Maiden Castle in Dorset.

It is still not known why these fortresses were built, and against what enemy they offered protection; or even, where the very large number of people needed adequately to defend the fortress would have come from.

There are more flint mines at Harrow Hill, which, with Cissbury, supplied flint

---

PLACES OF INTEREST AROUND WORTHING

Museum of Sussex Folklore, Tarring
A museum housed in a row of fifteenth-century cottages, which concentrates on the customs, and traditional beliefs of the county.

Chanctonbury Ring
Iron Age fort providing views into Hampshire, Surrey, and East Sussex. Crowned by a clump of beech trees.

Cissbury Ring
Neolithic flintmines, an Iron Age fort, and a viewpoint offering panoramic views including Chanctonbury.

Salvington Mill
A post mill of about 1700 with an unusual tail wheel.

Marlipins Museum, Shoreham
The history of Shoreham in a strange old twelfth-century building.

Shipley Mill
Known as King's Mill, this smock mill built in 1879 is a memorial to Hilaire Belloc.

Highdown Chalk Garden, Goring-by-Sea
A 5-acre garden wrought from a chalk pit.

artefacts to tribes all over Europe, and these areas have been christened the 'Sheffield of Flint'.

North of Harrow Hill on the A283, Storrington has been a settlement since prehistoric times, and a market town since 1399. There are old houses and quiet places if you leave the main street; Brewers Yard is a picturesque adaptation of a 400-year-old brewery.

About two miles west of Storrington stands Parham, reckoned by many to be the loveliest of the Sussex Elizabethan great houses. Superbly sited within a great park, it was rebuilt in 1577-80 by Sir Thomas Palmer, a wealthy mercer, who helped Drake singe the King of Spain's beard at Cadiz. Although the house is now closed to casual visitors, it is possible to visit by appointment, and the gardens are open to the public, including a four-acre walled garden, an eighteenth-century garden, a lake, and the park. The house contains the longest long gallery in England, and embroidery said to be by Mary Queen of Scots and her ladies. The pictures are superb, and in the north-east wing traces of the earlier fourteenth- and fifteenth-century building can still be seen.

The area bounded by the A272, A29, A24 and the A283, is one of those rural areas with small villages clustered around small churches, that caused visitors during the 1920s and 1930s to wax lyrical about our rustic heritage.

Shipley is thought to have been a medieval iron town, and the Templars had a monastery there. To the east of Shipley is Knepp Castle, designed by Nash in 1809, and rebuilt to look exactly the same after a fire in 1904. Remnants of William de Braose's castle stand in the grounds, and the lake, Knepp Mill

Steyning

Pond, is the largest in Sussex. Kings Mill is a smock windmill, built in 1879. Hilaire Belloc lived there, and called it 'Mrs Shipley'. It was restored in 1957, and is now his memorial, complete with an exhibition of his life and work.

Coolham is the location of the strangely named 'Blue Idol'. This beautiful old house, dating from the time of the Armada, was a Friends' Meeting House, and William Penn, who lived at Warminghurst, rode to Coolham to worship. West Chiltington three miles to the south-west retains its stocks and whipping post.

The road to Worthing passes through Findon, famous for its racing stables and sheep fair, and Salvington where there is a fine old post mill dating from about 1700.

Worthing has for many years been labelled an old people's town. But, while it will always be an excellent place for retirement, it is nevertheless a much more progressive resort than the image suggests. Worthing provides excellent recreational facilities, good shopping, first-class entertainment, and has taken active steps to ensure that it neither pollutes its own beaches, nor contaminates those of other seaside towns.

The town grew as a resort through the stimulus of developments at Brighton in the late eighteenth century, although the Romans had many villas in the area. It was not until 1797, when Princess Amelia became a counter-attraction to the Prince Regent, that the town really began to expand. Even so, it was a fairly slow advance, for by 1866 the population was still under 8,000, and only rose to 17,000 in the 1890s. The railway station was built in 1845, and the pier in 1868.

The changes in agricultural patterns brought about by the depression in farming during the 1870s established Worthing as an horticultural centre with vast areas under glass, which today grow flowers as well as salad vegetables. Highdown Gardens at Goring

King's Mill (Belloc's Mill), Shipley

demonstrates how well roses and spring bulbs grow in this area, and Hollygate Cactus Nurseries at Ashington use their glasshouses to produce thousands of species of rare cacti and succulents.

Oscar Wilde wrote *The Importance of Being Earnest* while staying here, and called the principal character John Worthing. If history had taken a different turn, he could have been called John Broadwater, because Broadwater was at one time the more important settlement, and the Transitional church is still the mother church of Worthing.

West Tarring was the site of a palace belonging to the Archbishop of Canterbury, usually referred to as Becket's Palace, although too recent to have been so. It is now the parish hall. The house opposite has fig trees supposedly established by Thomas à Becket, although others attribute them to St Richard of Chichester.

Parsonage Row is a beautiful timbered building of what is known as the wealden type. The whole structure was formerly 6, 8 and 10 High Street, but is now a single building housing a museum of Sussex folklore.

Sompting church has a unique cap on the tower known as a 'Rhenish Helm', from similar caps in the Rhineland. Part of the structure is reputed to date from 960, and it is certainly pre-Conquest. It passed to the Knights Templars in 1154, and shortly after they were suppressed in 1306, the church became the property of the Knights Hospitallers. The blocked door in the north wall is known as a Devil's Door. Although most of these are now filled in, they were once left open at baptisms to allow the child's evil spirits to depart. They were also used for baptismal processions and funerals.

Shoreham is now a thriving port carrying a tonnage nearly as great as that of Dover, and the town certainly dates back to Roman times. There is some controversy over whether Shoreham was *Portus Adurnii,* but this seems unlikely as the river does not appear to have been called Adur for that long. However, there was a Roman port in the Old Shoreham-Aldrington area, and several villas have been discovered in the vicinity. At one time Shoreham was a limb of Hastings in the Cinque Ports Confederation, and once again the connection with the Roman fleet is evident.

The present name derives from Scoreham, meaning 'The homestead on the sea shore', reflecting the Saxon re-naming of nearly every feature in Sussex. Around 1100, New Shoreham was designed because of the silting up of the old harbour, and during the twelfth and thirteenth centuries the new port became the most important cross channel point in the south of England. In 1199 King John landed with a large army on his way to Westminster to be crowned. A year later, he sailed from Shoreham to meet the French King. In 1305 Edward I was at the harbour; indeed most reigning monarchs from the time of Alfred have visited or used the port, and during the reign of Edward III, Shoreham furnished 26 ships and 239 sailors for the fleet that faced the French at Calais.

1651 saw the escape of Charles II from the port in the boat of Nicholas Tettersell (who is buried at Brighton). It is said that a sailor named Catt, when reproved for staring, remarked 'A Catt may look at a king', which is improbable enough to be true.

The quaint chequered building in the High Street now houses a museum, and is called 'The Marlipins', a name which apparently cannot be explained. It is believed that it has variously served as a store-house and a customs house. However, the generally ecclesiastical look of the building suggests that possibly the name, once written as Malduppine or Malduppynne, in fact derives from an old French word *malpeign* (a shabby fellow), implying a hospital or hospice for sick or poor travellers. There are certainly similarities to buildings of similar function in Canterbury and in France.

Both of Shoreham's churches are notable. St Nicholas in Old Shoreham is certainly pre-Conquest in part. St Mary de Haura, or St Mary of the harbour or haven, dates from about 1130, and the present building represents only part of the original church, the rest of which was demolished in 1480. Both churches were given to the abbey of Saumur in Anjou by William de Braose, and eventually became the property of Magdalen College, Oxford.

Old Shoreham bridge is a quaint wooden structure looking like scaffolding that fell over. It is visible from the A27, from where the chapel of Lancing College can also be seen. This great pseudo-gothic Victorian pile which has received much praise, was begun in 1867, and is still unfinished. However worthy the building may be in itself, it is completely out of character with its surroundings: it is a great disfigurement of the Downs by a minster-like lump which should be sent to some Victorian railway town where it belongs. The Romans, having more taste, built a temple on these slopes: would that it were there instead.

6 Around Arundel

The area dealt with in this chapter was originally within the Norman rape of Arundel, Chichester being separated at a later date. The combined rape was placed in the charge of Roger de Montgomery, a kinsman of the Conqueror who fought with distinction on Senlac Hill in 1066. Montgomery was created Earl of Arundel in 1067, and whosoever owns the castle is still so-styled.

Arundel Castle is possibly built on the site of a Saxon fort, but the earliest parts of the present building date from around 1070. The keep, known as Montgomery's Tower, was built at this time, so possibly was Gateway Chambers where Empress Matilda lived in 1139.

Roger's son Hugh died childless in 1094, and his brother, Robert de Belesme, was attainted after rebelling against Henry I. After a period of ownership by the crown, the castle and lands were bestowed upon the d'Aubigny family. William d'Aubigny married Adeliza of Louvain, the widow of Henry I. This brought about the visit

Arundel Castle

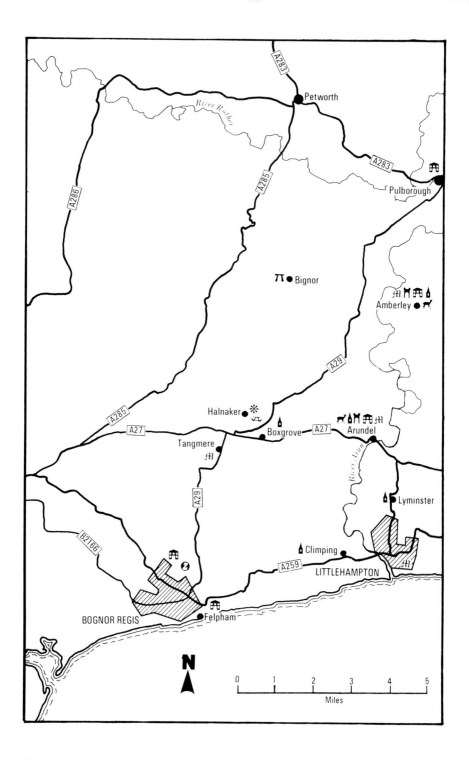

Sheffield Park Gardens

Sackville College, East Grinstead

Pool Bridge, Hartfield

Sompting Church

of Matilda a year later, to stay with her step-mother. This visit terminated abruptly when Stephen appeared with a siege-force, and Matilda retreated westwards.

In 1243, John Fitzalan inherited the castle through his mother, Isabel d'Aubigny, and in 1555 the last Fitzalan, Mary, married Thomas Fourth Duke of Norfolk, whose line have held the castle ever since. The Norfolks are the premier Dukes, and hold the post of Earl Marshal, among whose duties are the organisation of coronations and state events.

The castle has been besieged three times; in 1102 by Henry I, in 1139 by Stephen, and in 1643 by Sir William Waller. This last siege resulted in considerable damage, as the parliamentary troops mounted a cannon on the nearby church of St Nicholas, and pounded large parts of the castle into rubble. The present building dates in large part from the restoration and rebuilding carried out by Charles, the Eleventh Duke at the end of the eighteenth century and Henry the

---

PLACES OF INTEREST IN ARUNDEL

Arundel Castle
Fairytale seat of the Dukes of Norfolk, looming above the town like a castle in a story by the Brothers Grimm. Fine furniture, pictures, and objets d'art.

Museum of Curiosity
Much that is weird and some that is macabre in a glorious profusion of strange exhibits.

Toy Museum
Children's toys and small militaria.

Wildfowl Trust
Rare and exotic waterfowl on lakes set in water meadows. A peaceful and beautiful experience.

Fifteenth Duke, a century later. This should not be allowed to detract from a superb building however. Viewed from the A27, the castle rises above the town like something from Hans Anderson, or the Brothers Grimm, and, even at close quarters, the visitor half expects to see knights and damsels, or Rapunzel letting down her golden hair. To see open-air performances of Shakespeare plays performed in the tilting yard, during the Arundel Festival in August, is a magical experience.

The interior of Arundel Castle is worthy of some description. Entering by the simple Stone Hall note the rococo sleigh, the chests, and the Italian walnut chairs. Pass on to the magnificent Barons' Hall, as long as a football pitch. There are Gobelin tapestries, and paintings by Van Dyke, Claessins, Palmezzano, and Van der Meulen.

The picture gallery is a family history of the Arundels and the Norfolks, with fine work by Lely and Laurence. The Grand Staircase with its heraldic beasts bearing shields, and the Dining Room with its furniture, are especially fine, while the Drawing Room has simple charm amid grand surroundings.

The extensive grounds of the castle are beautiful and include the famous Swanbourne Lake, where it is possible to go boating. Bernard, the Sixteenth Duke, established the tradition of visiting test teams playing their first match in these grounds, on what is surely the most scenic cricket field in the world. The Duke (or Duchess) of Norfolk's XI always contains several Sussex players, so as to ensure a skilful and entertaining match.

A little further on from Swanbourne Lake, the Arundel Wildfowl Trust occupies an area of lakes and water meadows, where the visitor can view, from hides, a huge number of tame and wild water-fowl.

Near the bridge there are the ruins of a hospital or Maison Dieu, founded in 1395 for 'Twenty poor men, aged or infirm but of good life'. It was dissolved

Swanbourne Lake, Arundel

Maison Dieu, Arundel

Museum of Curiosity, Arundel

by Henry VIII, and while there may have been some justification for the dissolution of some monasteries and religious organisations, it is difficult to find any for this petty act.

The Museum of Curiosity is built around the macabre stuffed tableaux of Walter Potter which were formerly housed at Bramber. The schoolrooms of stuffed kittens and guinea-pigs, and the Death of Cock Robin with full personnel, have been supplemented with a glorious assembly of all that is weird and wonderful. Saws of swordfishes, two-headed piglets preserved in spirit, rodents with runaway teeth, strange objects of all times and types, are jumbled together in strange juxtaposition.

The Cathedral of Our Lady and St Philip Howard was formerly the church of St Philip Neri. It was built by the Fifteenth Duke between 1868 and 1873, and designed by Joseph Hansom, inventor of the hansom cab and architect of Birmingham Town Hall. It

is possible that the town hall is a slightly more attractive building, but certainly neither is attractive.

St Nicholas is unique in that it is both Church of England and Roman Catholic, divided by a glass screen. The style is Perpendicular, having been rebuilt around 1380, although the original church was probably Saxon, at least in part. The Fitzalan and Lady Chapels contain the tombs of the illustrious house of Fitzalan and Howard.

One of their servants was the legendary Bevis of Hampton, one-time warder at the castle, and a man of some stature. It is said that he ate an ox a week (with bread and mustard), and drank two hogsheads of beer. During his off-duty hours he used to walk across to the Isle of Wight, and when the strain of his irregular life took its toll, he flung his sword from the castle, asking to be buried where it fell. A prehistoric mound in Arundel Park is known as Bevis's Grave.

South of Arundel, Littlehampton is a seaside resort which, although pleasant enough, has seen better days. The harbour area is the best feature; the fishing is good, and the boat hire is brisk. Arundel mullet is a delicacy which with Amberley trout, Chichester lobster, and Selsey cockles, are Sussex offerings considered by many to be superior to all others. Although Littlehampton is a mainly Victorian town, it does in fact have its place in history. William Rufus landed here, and so did Queen Matilda. Warships were built here in the time of Henry VIII, while in later days sailing ships plied to Norway and Newcastle, Honfleur and Holland. French prisoners from the Battle of Crécy were put ashore at Littlehampton, and later French boats, eighty of them, were also imprisoned after being taken in the Channel.

There is a ferry to the golf links on the western bank of the Arun where there is a huge sandy beach with extensive dunes. Wildlife is varied and prolific, and ornithologists can observe oyster-catchers, sanderlings, turnstones, hobby, wheatear, even the occasional avocet; botanists can find orchids, houndstongue, tamarisks, and the strangely-named squinancy wort.

Lyminster, to the north of Littlehampton, dates from Saxon times, and once belonged to Alfred the Great. Traces of this Saxon origin can be seen in the church. The nave, chancel, and chancel arch, show this influence, and the church was a nuns' chapel in the time of Athelstan. Lyminster is famous for

Littlehampton Miniature Railway

the Knucker Hole, a deep pool fed by an underground spring. The word Knucker is derived from the Saxon word *nicor*, a water monster or water-dragon. According to legend it used to roam the surrounding countryside, devouring people and livestock, until slain by a passing knight, who thereby won the hand of the daughter of the King of Sussex.

Another notable church in this area is that at Climping. There is a saying in West Sussex about churches, which goes, 'Bosham for antiquity, Boxgrove for beauty, Climping for perfection', and indeed St Mary is a very fine example of an Early English Church, with a Transitional tower, the doorway of which has fine dog-tooth and chevron moulding reminiscent of the well-known doorways at Kilpeck in Herefordshire or Barfreston in Kent, although more simple. There is a fine old chest in this church, dating from the thirteenth century, with a slot for Peter's Pence.

Ford was actually once a Roman fording place across the river, and its church is small and partly Saxon. Nearby Yapton takes its name from Eappa, a companion of Wilfred, who established his cathedral at Selsey.

Felpham will be forever associated with William Blake who lived there for three years, working for his patron William Hayley, the poet. Blake wrote the words of 'Jerusalem'. He was a mystic, and in Felpham he claimed to have seen a fairies funeral. His beautiful cottage is still there, the subject of many photographs.

Bognor Regis obtained its suffix after King George V spent time there recuperating from an illness in 1928. The town escaped being called Hothampton, after Sir Richard Hotham, a London hatter, took over the small hamlet which existed in 1787, and began large scale development with a view to making Bognor a fasionable rival to Brighton. He also tried to change the name, but was unsuccessful with both ambitions, despite being successful in attracting

Princess Charlotte to the town. She stayed at Dome House, but finished up in Brighton. Dome House was built as a potential residence for George III, or the Prince Regent, but neither could be enticed. Hotham House was built, but Hothampton never became a reality.

There is the well-known story (probably apocryphal) that when George V was dying, an equerry suggested that he once again try the healing powers of Bognor, to which the king replied 'B----r Bognor'. Queen Victoria, on the other hand, referred to 'Dear little Bognor'. Nevertheless, for those who like an English seaside holiday, with sun, sea, and sand, Bognor is better than many, and as good as most. Sand there is in plenty, clean and flat, with safe swimming off a softly shelving beach in clean water.

Zootopia in Hotham Park should please the children, with its animals displayed amid creations of fantasy and fairy-tale. The whole area is now called Rainbow's End Family Adventure Park. This, combined with the multiplicity of attractions offered by Butlins, ensure that there is plenty of entertainment for all holidaymakers, and the surrounding countryside will delight their senses.

North of Bognor, Boxgrove Priory has a quiet beauty which stays fixed in the memory. It was built between the years 1115 and 1220 as a Benedictine house under the Abbey of Lessay near Cherbourg. It has been suggested that, such are the similarities between this building and Chichester Cathedral, that the same architect was responsible for both. The De La Warr chantry is justly famous, and there is a model of the priory as it was around 1250. The chancel is particularly fine, and the fifteenth-century galleries in the transepts are thought to be unique in England. The first recorded game of cricket in Sussex took place at Boxgrove in 1622, and the church wardens were reported as having been in trouble several times for playing during evensong and on Sundays in Boxgrove

Amberley

churchyard, 'Contrarie to the seventh article, and for that they use to breake windowes with the ball'.

On Halnaker Hill stands Halnaker windmill where it has stood since 1740. It is the oldest tower mill in Sussex, with an ogee cap and unusual tile hanging. This mill is visible from the sea, and is used as a landmark for coastal shipping. The name Halnaker, which is pronounced 'Hannaker', is probably derived from the Old English

Halganoecer, which became its modern form by late medieval times. This means 'saint's land'; St Wilfred was given the land by King Ethelwalch. The suggestion that it is a corruption of 'half-naked' is most unlikely.

North of Arundel lies Bignor which has a Roman villa of great size, dating from early in the second century. It was continually expanded over two hundred years, and the mosaics are known throughout the world; the Ganymede

---

PLACES OF INTEREST AROUND ARUNDEL

Bignor Roman Villa
Extensive villa with notably fine floors. The mosaic of Ganymede compares with any yet discovered.

Hardham Church
An ancient church widely renowned for its medieval murals.

Parham House and Gardens
An Elizabethan manor house with rare needlework, antiques, and paintings. Superb long gallery. The garden is eighteenth century with a 4-acre walled garden. The house is open by arrangement only.

Chalk Pits Museum, Amberley
Industrial archaeology presented where lime-burners once worked. Small railway, stationary engines, radios, a blacksmith's forge, a cobbler, a printer, a carpenter's workshop, a pottery, and more besides.

Climping Church
Early Norman, and reputed to be the most perfect in Sussex.

Denmans, Fontwell
Walled gardens, a gravel garden, and a natural layout of trees, climbing plants, and shrubs.

Amberley Castle

mosaic is particularly outstanding. The whole villa covered nearly five acres, one barn alone being about 20ft long, and various other buildings possibly gave accommodation to several hundred sheep, up to forty oxen, and up to a hundred cattle. It is believed that some two thousand acres were used as arable land, and possibly as much again was under grass. The villa seems to have been deserted some time after AD300, possibly due to apprehensions caused by Saxon raids on the coast, and the destruction of Fishbourne.

Bury was the home of John Galsworthy, who lived at Bury House, and the actress and entertainer Mabel Constanduros lived at Prattendens Cottage. Bury seems to have produced some very keen sportswomen; for instance in 1796, the married women of Bury defeated the single women at cricket to the extent of eighty runs, after which, uniting forces, they challenged any women's team in the county. Before that, in 1791, two ladies of Bury, weighing in under the names of Big Ben and Mendoza, engaged in a prize-fight before a large crowd.

Amberley is a village which is often described as 'too perfect', a description both impossible and inaccurate. It is indeed very attractive, and well tended, which is hardly something for which to

be criticized. The scene is truly idyllic, with the river flowing through water meadows, past thatched cottages in gentle lanes, guarded by a castle and a church. The downs rise on one side, while on the other side Amberley Wild Brooks provide a sanctuary for wildlife. The castle dates in its earliest parts from about 1140, the great hall from 1350, and the crenellation from 1379. It was formerly a palace of the Bishop of Chichester, and never experienced hostilities. Indeed, apart from a one night stay by Charles II in 1651, the castle has not been famous in history. A manor house and a church complete the traditional village grouping. The church of St Michael is Norman, with later alterations, and the manor house is Tudor, built by Bishop Sherborne.

The South Downs Way passes Amberley, enabling the walkers to look down onto the Chalk Pits Museum. To describe this museum is difficult, purely because the organisers are always improving and adding to the exhibits. However, there is a radio museum, stationary engines, a topless Southdown bus dating from the time when the words 'bus service' also meant carrying parcels, making unscheduled stops, and knowing the customers. There are exhibitions devoted to line-burning, wealden iron, geology, an audio-visual centre, and a recently acquired industrial steam locomotive with track. Altogether, Chalk Pits Museum provides a broad spectrum of the industrial history of the South of England.

Amberley Wild Brooks is a nature reserve, maintained by the Sussex Trust for Nature Conservation. Although not open to the general public, the trust is very understanding, and will make arrangements for any genuine naturalist who wishes to visit. The Brooks usually flood in winter, and Amberley people are said to have webbed-feet.

Houghton Bridge and Stopham Bridge are both medieval, and extremely photogenic. Stopham was built in 1309, and Houghton, built by the Bishops of Chichester to aid progress to their castle, dates from around the same period. Stopham church is an amalgam of architectural styles from Saxon to Perpendicular, and the brasses of the Barttelot family are notable. There are eight, from John and Joan, 1428, to the daughters of Walter and Mary, 1626.

Hardham was for a while the home of an unknown artist who painted the murals in the church. They are of 'The Last Supper', 'The Adoration of the Magi', 'The Flight Into Egypt', 'The Massacre of Innocents', 'The Salutation of Elizabeth', 'Lazarus', 'Adam and Eve with the Serpent', and 'St George at the Battle of Antioch'. These murals were possibly painted when the church was built, soon after the Conquest, and this little church, standing close to the street, is probably the earliest picture gallery in England. In 1926 the pre-Roman occupation of Hardham was proved, and a Roman posting station of about AD 150 discovered.

Pulborough was first settled by the Romans who needed to guard this strategic point where Stane Street crossed the Arun. Parts of villas have been discovered at Borough Farm and Wynchford Bridge, and remains of a temple and a mausoleum along Stane Street. Pulborough was mentioned in the Domesday survey as *Polberge,* and was conferred upon Roger de Montgomery by William the Conqueror. There are several interesting buildings. The Oddfellows Arms is a tile-hung inn of considerable age, and Old House on Church Hill is a marvel of tumbling angles and quaintness. North of the village, the unusual tower standing on a knoll is called the Toat Monument or Tower, a folly built to commemorate one Samuel Drinkald, who fell from his horse and died there in 1823. Local tradition asserts that he and his horse were both buried beneath the tower, upside down. There was a belief among country people that on the Day of Judgement, the whole world would be turned topsy-turvy, and so those buried upside down would come up topsides on the great day, as reflected in the numerous inn signs for pubs called 'The World Turned Upside Down'.

Pulborough Church has a lych-gate. These covered churchyard gateways originally provided shelter for shrouded bodies, and later became a resting place for coffins while awaiting the priest. The church itself is mainly Perpendicular in style, and much of it can be dated to the years 1420-30.

Fittleworth has an old bridge, probably built in the seventeenth century, and a coaching inn which was originally two fourteenth-century cottages. The Swan has been an inn for centuries, and complaints about modernisation have been made from time to time, but each alteration becomes, in future years, something to be preserved. Sir Edward Elgar lived just outside the village, in a house called 'Brinkwells', and wrote his cello concerto here. Also, just outside Fittleworth there is a watermill with an iron waterwheel which no longer turns. It was working when Elgar was composing nearby in 1921, and may yet do so again.

7 From Chichester to the Hampshire Border___

According to Dr Curwen (an eminent local historian) Chichester was founded by a migration from the Trundle, an Iron Age hillfort, dating from about 250BC, overlaying an older Neolithic causewayed camp. Chichester was perhaps the first Roman military city in England. They called it *Regnum* or *Noviomagus*. Originally, the Romans used *Noviomagus*, or 'new city on the plain', but this was soon changed to *Regnum* in honour of King Cogidubnus, a life-long ally, who was highly regarded in Rome and made an Imperial Legate.

The walls of the city were built about AD200, and the streets still have the Roman configuration within them. Chichester was a principal city under the Romans for three hundred years, and was even mentioned in the writings of Ptolemy. There was an amphitheatre, now built over, some 100yd south-east of the city wall. It was discovered in 1935, and excavations revealed a stone wall, 10-12ft high, plastered and painted to resemble marble, and enclosing an area of 185ft by 150ft. It was said after the site had been built on that: 'The

The Cloisters, Chichester Cathedral

105

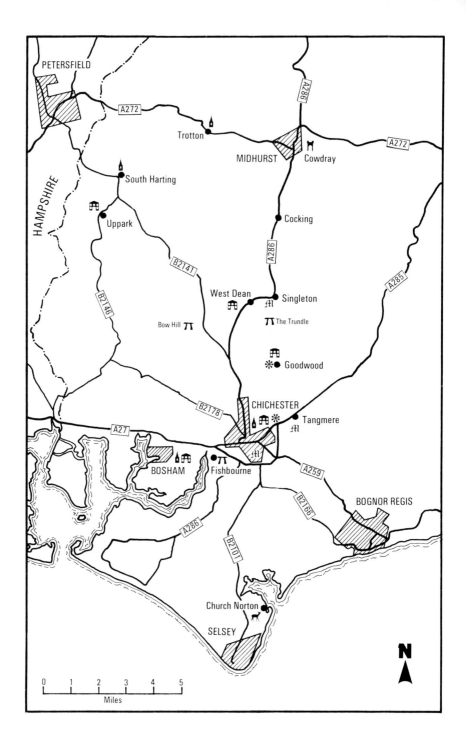

vandals could not find it in their hearts or purses to spare the only known Roman amphitheatre in the County of Sussex.' There is a piece of a basilica on view inside the cathedral, and a great deal of Roman *Regnum* remains to be explored whenever opportunity occurs.

Aella the Saxon arrived in 477, and his son Cissa made his headquarters in the city, giving it the present name of *Cissasceastre* or Cissa's stronghold. Chichester became an important market town, and by the time of Athelstan, possessed a mint.

St Wilfred, who landed at Selsey in 681, succeeded in converting the South Saxons to Christianity, and King Ethelwalch endowed him with lands.

The Danes attacked the city unsuccessfully in 895, and with more success in 994 and 1000. This period of uncertainty and fear was finally ended when the Witan chose Canute to be king in 1016, so putting an end to Danish raids.

Following the Conquest, the Rape of Chichester was given to Roger de Montgomery, and by 1075 the Bishopric was transferred from Selsey. Bishop Ralph de Luffa (1091-1123), energetically pursued the construction of the cathedral, and although work was delayed by a fire in 1114, much of the building was complete in 1123. It was based on the Abbaye aux Hommes at Caen. Bishop Seffrid II (1188-1204), undertook further work in 1187, after a fire destroyed the roof. He employed stone vaulting, and added a clerestory, as well as the two-bay retro-choir.

St Richard was Bishop from 1245 to 1253, and upon his canonisation in 1262, his body, which had lain near the Chapel of St Thomas and St Edmund, was translated to the retro-choir. Edward I was the most notable of the many pilgrims who came to worship at the shrine. Although destroyed during the reign of Henry VIII, the shrine has once again become a focus of veneration.

St Richard — Richard of Wych — was born at Droitwich in 1197, son of a yeoman. A humble and devout man, he often went on foot around his diocese, and lived a life both austere and simple. Unlike many saints in the panoply this man was simple, good, and most important, real and believable. Compare this exemplary saint with, for instance, St Rumwold, who was supposedly born able to preach, and died after three days. During this time he had even directed which churches should hold his relics!

The campanile, or detached bell-tower, was built in 1436, and is unique, as no other medieval cathedral has a

---

PLACES OF INTEREST IN CHICHESTER

Cathedral
A peaceful building ranging from Norman to Perpendicular in style. There is a shrine to St Richard, Romanesque carvings, a window by Chagall, and a tapestry by Piper. The campanile is unique.

St Mary's Hospital
An almshouse of thirteenth-century origins with strikingly good misericords.

Market Cross
Probably the best in Britain. Presented in sixteenth century by Bishop Storey.

Pallant House
A fine art gallery known locally as the 'Dodo House' from the weird birds in the gateposts.

Festival Theatre
A superb theatre featuring all the leading personalities in the performing arts. Famous festival each year featuring major plays.

Fishbourne Roman Palace
Palace of King Cogidubnus and the largest Roman residence found in Britain. Superb mosaic floors.

detached bell tower standing. It mounts eight bells, the oldest of which is dated 1583.

The Baptistry contains a memorial to William Collins, a poet who died in 1769, and the painting of the Baptism of Christ by Hans Feibusch. St George's Chapel has been the Regimental Chapel of the Royal Sussex Regiment since 1921. The plaque by the steps to the south transept commemorates Dr Bell, a highly-respected, greatly-loved, kind and gentle man, who was bishop from 1929-58.

There is an amusing little oddity decorating the corbel table above Langton's great window in the south transept. For those whose eyes are equal to the task, the personalities portrayed from west to east are: Mr Baldwin, Mr Parsons (foreman), Cecil Norman (builder), Mr Johnson (surveyor), Canon Mortlock, the Rt Rev Southwell (precentor), the Very Rev Duncan-Jones (dean), King George V, the Rt Rev Hordern (treasurer), the Rt Rev Dr Bell (bishop), Bishop Langton, the Ven B. Hoskyns (archdeacon), Dr Campbell (chancellor), Dr Harvey Grace (organist), and Ramsey MacDonald. This pleasant little conceit was carved during a restoration in 1932.

The south choir aisle is notable for the panels of 1125 or earlier; 'The Raising of Lazarus', and 'Christ Arriving at Bethany being greeted by Mary and Martha', which could be early enough to have been salvaged from the earlier cathedral at Selsey. It is in this that aisle part of a Roman mosaic is exposed.

The Lady Chapel contains what is generally believed to be the tomb of Bishop Luffa (already mentioned as the builder), while the choir contains the Sherburne Screen, a tapestry by John Piper with motifs of the elements; earth, air, fire and water; the Trinity occupying the centre panels, and emblems of the evangelists . The north aisle contains the tomb of Richard Fitzalan, Earl of Arundel, who was beheaded by Richard II in 1397. It became commonly believed

that the head of the earl had miraculously reunited with his trunk, and this belief became so strong that eventually the king caused the tomb to be reopened.

At the western end of the outer aisle there is a statue in Roman dress. It represents William Huskisson, former MP for Chichester, who holds the doubtful distinction of being the first man to be killed by a train. This happened at the opening of the Liverpool and Manchester Railway in 1830.

It is possible to visit the library by special appointment. The core of the collection is the Latin books, originally numbering about 900 volumes of sixteenth- and seventeeth-century origin. Among the precious and interesting possessions are a missal bearing the signature of Archbishop Cranmer, and a book printed by Wynkyn de Worde, who used a block made by Caxton on the title page bearing the initials 'W.C.'. There is also a copy of the black-letter Bishop's Bible of 1595, commonly known as a 'Breeches Bible' from the rendering of Genesis iii,7, which runs 'They sewed figge-tree leaves together, and made themselves breeches'.

In 1861 the cathedral spire fell down, but by 1866 a perfect replica had been erected under the guidance of Sir Gilbert Scott, who was also responsible for the Albert Memorial and St Pancras Station in London.

The quality which strikes most people is the atmosphere of peace and gentleness inside the cathedral. On a summer day, with the doors open, the sunlight streaming in, and calls of rooks and jackdaws emphasising the stillness, the spirit of St Richard is all around, and there can be few places more completely in keeping with their purpose. To quote the local guide: 'The note of friendly informality continues in the Cathedral Close. It is pleasantly integrated into the life of the town. Shoppers take a short cut through medieval archways, students sunbathe on the grass outside the Lady

been well used, to judge from the wearing of the stone seats, by generations. It was a gift of lasting enrichment to Chichester — it is the finest market cross of its kind in England. Bishop Story also endowed the Prebendal School in West Street, where the cathedral choristers are educated.

Chichester saw much action in the Civil War, and it was besieged by Sir William Waller in 1642, before he went on to besiege Arundel Castle. The parliamentary forces did considerable damage while quartered in the city after the eight-day siege ended, and this, combined with the bombardment, and demolition by the defenders, resulted in

The Market Cross, Chichester

Chichester

Chapel, busy figures crouch over their hobby at the Brass Rubbing Centre, friends meet for coffee at the restaurant off the cloisters. It is a good place for a quiet stroll, a maze of high flint walls, and little flowery cottages, and tempting glimpses of secret walled gardens — the result of centuries of haphazard growth, and an unanswerable refutation of the pretensions of modern 'planners'. In the furthest corner of the Close, against the city wall, the garden of the Bishop's palace is open to the public, a haven of eighteenth century tranquillity.'

At the centre of the city the Market Cross stands as a memorial to Bishop Story. He made a gift of the cross to the city in 1501, to be used for the benefit of people attending the market, and it has

a decline in fortunes, which was not reversed until the eighteenth century; the subsequent surge in building activity giving the city its Georgian appearance.

Several noteworthy buildings were erected during this period. The Butter Market in North Street was built in 1808 to a design by Nash to replace the market cross as accommodation for small traders. In the area of the Pallants, so named from the Latin *Palantia*, signifying exclusive jurisdiction or 'palantine' rights, Pallant House stands at the crossing of the four Pallants, built in 1712, and is now an art gallery. It is known locally as 'The Dodo House' because of the peculiar avian appendages on the gateposts. They were part of the crest of one Henry 'Lisbon' Peckham, a wine merchant, and should have been ostriches, and would have been had anyone known what ostriches looked like.

The Ship Hotel in North Street was built by Admiral Sir George Murray in 1790. He commanded the leading ship of Nelson's squadron at the Battle of Copenhagen in 1801. General Eisenhower stayed there in 1944.

There are of course many much older buildings in Chichester. St Mary's Hospital in St Martin's Square probably dates from about 1285, when the Greyfriars moved to Priory Park. The hospital was built to provide refuge for thirteen aged people of good life and religious observance, as well as 'The friendless sick and impoverished travellers'.

St Olave Church in North Street is now a book shop. It is certainly Saxon, and perhaps even Roman, in origin, but it was extensively rebuilt in the thirteenth and fourteenth centuries. There is a distinct likelihood that this church was built for, or by, Danish merchants who had settled in the city for some time before the Conquest; hence the dedication. St Olave, Olaf, or Olaf the Thick, was an exceedingly energetic agent of Christian conversion, not above hanging, blinding, or mutilating anyone wanting to remain heathen. For such zeal he was canonised, and his relics are in the cathedral at Trondheim.

Also in North Street, the Council Chamber has an entrance which projects, on pillars, beyond the building. It was built in 1731, and displays the famous Neptune and Minerva stone recording the dedication of a Roman Temple. The assembly room at the rear of the chamber was designed by Wyatt and built in 1783.

*The Council House,
Chichester*

North Street leads to Oaklands Park where theatre lovers will wish to visit the Festival Theatre, whose first director was Sir Laurence Olivier. It was completed in 1962, and from the first has presented all that is good and all who are great in theatre and the performing arts. There can scarcely be a famous stage performer who has not appeared on the Festival Theatre's open stage. The season of plays runs from May to September — when plays are not being performed, singers and musicians, both jazz and classical are invited to perform, making this a truly international centre of the first rank.

In the literary world also, Chichester has been associated with some famous names. John Keats began to write *The Eve of St Agnes* while staying at Eastgate Square. Edward Fitzgerald, translator of the *Rubiáyát of Omar Khaayyám* was married in the city, and a Dean of Chichester, John William Burgon, wrote the poem 'Petra', which contains the immortal line 'A rose-red city, half as old as time'. Anna Sewell, who wrote *Black Beauty*, made her home here; Gustav Holst, the composer, is buried in the cathedral; Eric Gill, the artist and sculptor, lived in the city as a boy, and later executed two memorials which can be seen in the cathedral transept.

About a mile and a half from Chichester, westwards along the A27, stands a small village called Fishbourne. Until fairly recently, the name meant little to anyone, but when in 1960 a workman found pieces of mosaic among his diggings, Fishbourne Roman Palace was discovered. Believed to be the palace of Tiberius Claudius Cogidubnus, Imperial Legate, and King of the Belgae, these remains represent the largest Roman residence yet rediscovered in Britain, covering almost seven acres. It was built soon after AD43, in a style more common in Italy, with more than sixty rooms around the central courtyard or garden. The north wing, now under cover, has many fine mosaics, including one of a boy on a dolphin, which design is becoming associated with Sussex rather in the way

All Saints' Church, East Dean

Hypocaust at Fishbourne Roman Palace

that the oasthouse has become the symbol of Kent. There is another pavement showing cupid gladiators, although the limitations of the medium render their faces positively senile. A reconstruction of a dining room shows what one room may have looked like around AD100, and the gardens have been replanted to a plan of about the same period, using plants believed to have been grown at that time.

The palace was destroyed by fire in about AD280, probably as a result of a Saxon raid. A body of a man who apparently perished in the raid can still be seen, although the body could have been buried at a later date. After the destruction, the owners returned to search the débris for anything they could salvage. The disturbance they made could still be traced during the excavation. Later the palace walls were

PLACES OF INTEREST AROUND CHICHESTER

Bosham Church
Saxon church on Roman foundations. Canute's daughter is buried here.

Boxgrove Priory
Beautiful church with the famous De La Warr tomb and chapel.

Bignor Roman Villa
Large villa with fine mosaics.

Chilsdown Vineyard, Singleton
Thirteen-acre vineyard set in the South Downs around a former railway station.

Goodwood House
Ancestral home of the Dukes of Richmond and Gordon. Superb collection of paintings, furniture, and family mementoes.

Halnaker Mill
The oldest tower mill in Sussex perched high on a hill with stunning views.

Rose Centre, Apuldram Manor
20,000 roses of 100 named varieties.

Tangmere Museum of Military Aviation
Relics, maps, photographs, medals, and uniforms of World War II.

Weald and Downland Museum, Singleton
A fascinating collection of re-erected, rescued buildings on a beautiful site.

West Dean Gardens
A 35-acre garden partly designed by Gertrude Jekyll.

The Trundle
Massive iron age hillfort.

dismantled to foundation level, and all the useful building material was removed to be used elsewhere, probably in Chichester or in neighbouring villas. The site became forgotten and reverted to farmland. In the Middle Ages, the fields were ploughed, but happily the remains have been discovered and have become one of the most important Roman sites in Europe.

South of the A27, between Chichester and the Hampshire border, lies the Selsey peninsula, and the creeks and inlets around Thorney Island and Bosham. The Selsey peninsula has about it something of the atmosphere of the Romney Marsh or the Pevensey flats; a quality of the light perhaps, or a similarity of plant life. Selsey was where Wilfred, Bishop of Northumbria established his ministry to convert the South Saxons, after his explusion from the north. The saint established a monastery in 681, which is thought to have stood where Church Norton stands today. It is recorded by Edda in his *Vita Wilfredi* that the missionaries found the Saxons very difficult to convert, and that the saint found the way to their souls through their stomachs by teaching them to fish at a time of famine. That coast-dwellers in Sussex at any time should have been lacking in such knowledge is hard to credit. Not that St Wilfred appeared as a shining example to all men, for he has been authoritatively represented as an ambitious and self-seeking man. He did, however, establish a cathedral at Selsey which was transferred to Chichester in 1075, partly as a result of damage caused by the encroachment of the sea on the peninsula. The cathedral is now somewhere under the sea (as is a complete deer park), and local tradition maintains that the bells of the sunken cathedral may be heard ringing at times of abnormally low tide. This folk legend is all that remains of St Wilfred in Sussex, because in all the county not one church is dedicated to him; there is not even a chapel in Chichester Cathedral.

Bosham Church

At Church Norton, the old rectory is believed to occupy the site of St Wilfred's College of Canons. It stands by the mouth of Pagham Harbour, which did not exist until recently. In 1910, the sea swallowed all the land which had been reclaimed in that area, and more. The shore at Bracklesham regularly yields fossils, Saxon and Celtic jewellery, and Roman coins from land long since engulfed by the sea. Pagham Harbour, however, is an area of exceptional interest for birdwatchers and other naturalists. There is a footpath round the shore, and an interpretation centre at Sidlesham, and most birds which wade, paddle, swim or fish can be observed regularly here.

At Earnley the smock mill is thought to have been built in 1827, incorporating earlier machinery. Nearby West Wittering has another tall structure, called the Cakeham Tower. It was built by Bishop Sherburne to enable him to contemplate the view. There is another tower at Apuldram, not Tudor as is Cakeham, but early fifteenth century. It seems that one Ryman felt that a castle would be a desirable place to live, but the king, Henry VI, while not questioning the desirability of castles in general, pointedly questioned the desirability of Ryman having one at Apuldram. Having only completed the tower, Ryman placated the king by donating the rest of the stone for the building of the campanile at Chichester Cathedral.

Bosham is the oldest site of Christianity in Sussex, where men have worshipped since before St Augustine came to Canterbury — more than 1,600 years ago. The ancient church is Saxon on Roman and British foundations. The chancel arch is Saxon, and at its foot are the stones of the original Roman Basilica of AD350. To the right is the tomb of the daughter of King Canute, buried there in 1020. At the centre, immediately below the pavement, lie two stone coffins discovered in 1944, one probably containing the bones of Earl Godwin. Still further to the right is the alleged site of Dicul's Cell, where he and five brethren 'served the Lord'. Dicul was a Hibernian monk who was endeavouring to convert the Saxons of the area before the advent of St Wilfred.

The font is stapled to enable it to be locked, to prevent the Holy Water being stolen by witches for spells, or for the celebration of Black Mass. There are pilgrims' and crusaders' marks on two of the pillars, Bosham being a port of embarkation for the Continent. Harold Godwinsson sailed from Bosham on the ill-fated voyage that led to his capture by William the Conqueror, and his swearing a contentious oath of fealty. These scenes are depicted in the Bayeaux Tapestry.

Vespasian made his camp at Bosham, using it for his campaign to take the Isle of Wight and the West. Vespasian established his camp around AD44-5 commanding the Second Legion, known as the Augusta. On his western campaign he possibly had additional assistance from elements of the Fourteenth Legion, the Gemina, and the Twentieth Legion, the Valeria. After the successful completion of the invasion, the Roman army left government to a civil administration, and the area prospered for nearly three hundred years.

By AD477, the Romans had gone, and the Romano-British faced the onslaught of the Saxons under Aella, who with his sons, Cissa, Wlencing, and Cymen, conquered the South and slaughtered the native Britons at a final battle at Anderida. The period after this, the Dark Ages, is only illuminated occasionally, such as upon the arrival of St Wilfred, or the raid of the Danes in

AD895. It is said that they stole the bells of Bosham Church, but that the weight of them capsized their longships. Now, when the new bells ring, it is said that the old ones under the sea chime in reply.

At Bosham Canute attempted, unsuccessfully, to reclaim the land. As in this part of Sussex a mud bank erected to keep out the sea during land reclamation is known as a 'chair' Canute's activities have been misinterpreted to become the popular legend that he put a chair on the beach and forbade the tide rise any further.

Bosham (pronounced Bozzum) has a Tudor and Jacobean manor house, which is believed to stand on the site of the palace of Canute. It is also believed to stand on Cavalier treasure buried

Watermill at Bosham

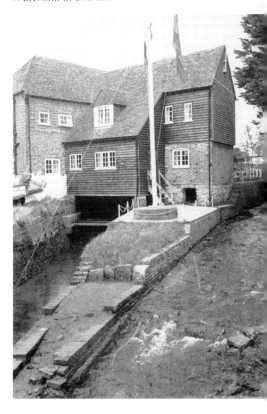

115

The Tapestry Room, Goodwood House

during the Civil War, and to have (of course) a secret tunnel. It is said with some justification that at high tide Bosham is a fine lady, but at low tide, a slut.

North of Chichester and the A27 lie Goodwood House and Singleton. Goodwood House is the home of the Dukes of Richmond and Gordon, and has been since the First Duke purchased the original building for £4,100 in 1697, for use as a hunting lodge. The original house was built about 1590, and was rebuilt in 1617 by the Ninth Earl of Northumberland. Goodwood House is today largely as created by the Third Duke, who was also responsible for the building of the Martello towers along the coast. He commissioned James

Wyatt to build a grandiose octagon with a tower at each corner. Only three sides were completed, but even so, the expense proved so great that the duke left liabilities of some £150,000 at his death.

Four years before he died, the duke started horse racing, and in 1802 'Glorious Goodwood' was born on what is arguably the most beautiful racecourse in the world. The motor-racing circuit was established by the present duke using the war-time Westhampnett Airfield. Top class racing took place during 1948-66, until rising speeds rendered the course potentially dangerous to spectators. It is still used for testing, training, trials, and rallies.

Within the house all is gracious, spacious, and beautiful. The Round

Reception Room contains a portrait by Lely of Frances Theresa Stewart, later Duchess of Richmond, posing as Minerva. This portrait was the basis of Britannia, who has appeared on coins and banknotes ever since. The Ballroom contains a portrait by Van Dyck of Charles I and Queen Henrietta Maria, and other paintings of the royal children by the same artist; Charles, later Charles II, was the father of the First Duke.

The Yellow Drawing Room contains many fine pieces collected by the Third Duke. There is an exceptionally fine display of Sèvres porcelain. The Card Room is thought by many to be the loveliest room in Goodwood House; again it has Sèvres porcelain and French furniture. The Main Hall contains a picture of the Thames from Richmond House by that great Italian master, Canaletto, and the Long Hall contains three famous pictures by Stubbs. There are Gobelin tapestries, furniture, and pictures, of superb quality at every turn, but this is no museum. It is light, airy, and it shines with care and pride. There cannot be many great houses which are so impressive and yet so intimate, breathtaking yet not overwhelming, and it is easy to see why the whole entity,

house and staff, radiates quiet pride.

Overlooking the Goodwood estate, The Trundle hillfort had been occupied for over 2,000 years when the Romans landed. The configuration is of three concentric rings, the inner Neolithic, the outer Iron Age. Flint mines were worked around 2000BC, and excavations have produced the skeleton of a woman, aged about twenty-five, buried in the crouching position adopted during that period. The objects recovered included the bones of horned sheep, oxen, pigs, and dogs, as well as rare pottery and snail shells indicating an extremely wet climate.

Singleton is the home of the Weald and Downland Museum, founded in 1966, and opened to the public in 1971. The main purpose of the museum is to rescue good examples of vernacular architecture. Buildings which cannot be preserved *in situ* are dismantled and re-erected on this forty-acre site. It is hoped that eventually the museum will possess examples showing the development of traditional building from medieval times until the nineteenth century in the Weald and the Downland areas of Sussex. The museum is now taking on the appearance of an idyllic rustic village; an

A lane near Goodwood

impression which is enhanced by the demonstration of traditional crafts and skills. Charcoal burning, a smithy, a sawpit, wheelwrights, and potters, all blend with ancient granaries, a watermill, old cottages and barns, stables and farm buildings.

Bow Hill, west of the A286 near West Stoke, is by local tradition the site of a victory by the Saxons over the Danes, and the two long barrows have always been thought to contain the bodies of the defeated Danes. It is also believed that the yew grove was planted to commemorate the famous victory. Following the principle that there is some truth in any local tradition, it is possible that the yews were in fact planted for this reason, and that the Danes were put in a mass grave somewhere near, or even under the yews. The barrows of course pre-date this period by 2,000 years, and there are other Neolithic traces; flint mines, linchets, a causeway, and ramparts, which prove that this was an important prehistoric site. Further evidence of the importance of this area can be seen at Stoke Down and Stoughton Down.

Cocking has a curious piece of doggerel which springs from age-old weather lore. From beech-woods on the Downs, there sometimes rises a mist which rolls down the hillsides like chimney-smoke. This mist has the strange name of 'Foxes Brewings', and if it travels towards Cocking, rain will follow, as recorded in the rhyme:
'When Foxes Brewings go to Cocking
Foxes Brewings come back dropping.'
No-one seems to have established how 'Foxes Brewings' originated as a phrase, but my suggestion is that it is a Sussex corruption from the French. *Faux Bruine* would literally be 'false rain' or 'false drizzle' which would seem to be appropriate both for the sound and for the weather content. Unfortunately, various authorities have tried to translate Sussex dialect into 'correct English' from imperfect knowledge, thus

Watermill at Weald and Down Open Air Museum, Singleton

resulting in further corruption. A classic example of this is the Keddle net, which is pegged out on Sussex beaches to trap fish as the tide retreats. Because the Sussex dialect transforms a double 'T' sound into a double 'D' sound, it has been assumed by many authorities that Keddle represented Kettle, and a mythology of a weird practice of Sussex fishermen boiling their catch in fish kettles was born.

The nearby Cowdray estate owns a large amount of property in this area, which may be identified by the piercingly garish yellow paint, seemingly beloved by the estate owners, which fails completely to blend into the landscape.

The minor road which winds and twists towards Petersfield passes through a string of small flint and thatch downland villages. The first of these is Bepton, which has a small Early English church with a canopied tomb of good decorated work. Didling Church is of the same period.

South Harting is justly regarded as one of the most beautiful villages in Southern England. Timber and plaster cottages scatter along narrow lanes with the Western Rother to the north, and stately Uppark on the southern slopes. Anthony Trollope, author of *Barchester Towers*, lived in South Harting, and here he conceived the idea of introducing pillar-boxes into England. Gilbert White the naturalist, and John Caryll the poet, also lived in the village.

The Church of St Mary and St Gabriel is Early English, cruciform with a copper-clad spire, and a whipping-post and stocks for the ungodly, outside. Whipping-posts and stocks were often placed by churches as a sort of practical lesson in the rewards of heaven and of sin. East Harting also claims to have had a witch, Mother Digby, who had the ability to transform herself into a hare, although why she did this is not recorded.

Uppark once had H. G. Wells's mother as housekeeper, and it is generally accepted that 'Bladesover' in *Tono-Bungay* is Uppark, and that 'Wimblehurst' is Midhurst. The house was built around 1690 by the architect William Talman, who also designed Chatsworth House in Derbyshire. Humphrey Repton made some alterations in 1810. It was built for Sir Edward Ford, son of the Defender of Arundel Castle during the siege by Sir William Waller. A former owner, Sir Harry Fetherstonhaugh, used to make his fifteen-year-old mistress dance on a table for his guests. The table is still there and the mistress eventually danced into the affections of Lord Nelson; she was Emma Hart, later Lady Hamilton.

Uppark was offered to the Duke of Wellington, but having viewed its situation, 600ft up on the Downs, he declined the offer, saying that he feared the effect on his horses. He added, in his characteristically gracious manner that he 'Had already crossed the Alps once'. The house is now owned by the National Trust, and still contains many of its original wallpapers and fabrics. The bed used by the Prince Regent is on view, and there is a magnificent Queen Anne dolls' house.

The B2146, going south, passes through Lordington and Racton. Lordington House was the birthplace of the last Roman Catholic Archbishop of Canterbury, Cardinal Pole. Born in 1500, he was son of the Earl and Countess of Salisbury. Cardinal Pole (and his mother) criticised Henry VIII over the Act of Supremacy, designed to make the king head of the English Church. Cardinal Pole subsequently worked hard to effect a reconciliation between Catholic and Protestant theologians, but Henry had the countess executed. It is alleged that her ghost still walks the house displaying her cut throat.

Racton was the house of the Gunter family. Colonel Gunter was responsible for shepherding Charles II out of England. The village is also the home of the Racton Tower, a folly built in 1772 as an observation tower for the Third Earl of Halifax. It is said that he plied excise officers with strong drink and then signalled the all-clear to smugglers when they were drunk. The same earl donated the church tower at Westbourne near Emsworth, not, it is to be hoped, for the same purpose.

8 Inland Sussex (West)

The church of St George at Trotton was built around 1300, and soon after, in 1310, a brass was laid to Lady Margaret Camoys, the oldest brass of a woman in Britain. Lady Elizabeth Camoys was the widow of Hotspur, and was Shakespeare's 'Gentle Kate'. Her husband, Thomas, Baron Camoys, was a hero of Agincourt. He and his wife have a magnificent altar-tomb with very fine canopied brasses. Sir Thomas, Jnr, restored the church in 1400, and it is said that he also built the beautiful medieval bridge spanning the Western Rother. The church contains fourteenth-century frescoes at its west end. They are of the Seven Deadly Sins, and the Seven Acts of Mercy, with the figures of Moses and

the Lord. Other paintings depict the legends of St Hubert and St George, the patron saint of England.

Thomas Otway, playwright and tragic poet, son of a Rector of Woolbeding, was born in Trotton in 1651, and died in poverty in 1685. He is buried at St Clement Danes, but there is a tablet with a Latin inscription recording his life, affixed to a wall by the pulpit in St George's Church.

John Talbot White admirably sums up Midhurst: 'Midhurst, situated like Petworth on the green sand ridge, bears much the same relationship to the Cowdray estate as Petworth does to its big house. A Norman motte stands to the east of the church, the site of the

Midhurst

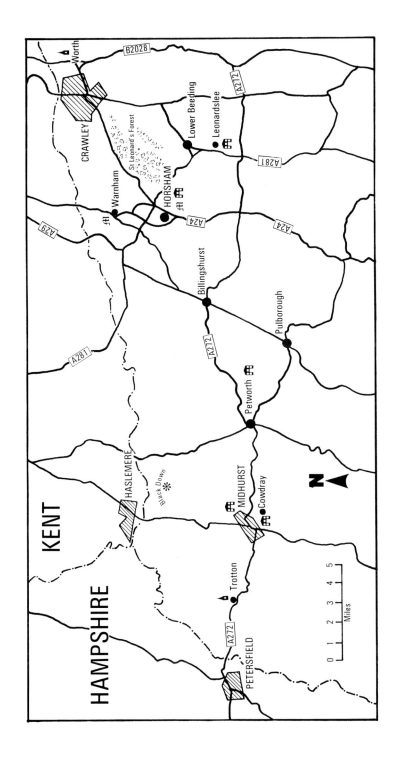

castle until the imposing Tudor house was built down by the river. The entry from the south crosses a ponded river and is immediately confronted with a mid-row of houses, including a sixteenth-century timbered Market House. The market place itself is merely a space in front of the church. In an endless fascination of old street names like Sheep Lane, Wool Lane and Knockhundred Row.

The two famous inns in Midhurst are the Angel and the Spread Eagle, the latter a fifteenth-century building nominated by Hilaire Belloc as, '. . . the oldest and most revered of all the prime inns of the world.' The famous

---

PLACES OF INTEREST IN AND AROUND MIDHURST

Blackdown, near Haslemere
The highest point in Sussex rising to over 900ft.

Burton Watermill, Petworth
A working watermill built in 1784.

Cowdray Park, Midhurst
Ruins of Sir Anthony Browne's Tudor mansion, near the world famous polo ground.

Petworth House (NT)
Paintings by Turner, carvings by Grinling Gibbons, park by Capability Brown.

Trotton Church and Bridge
The church has a brass to Lady Margaret Camoys dating from 1310, the oldest to a woman in Britain. The bridge is medieval and extremely picturesque.

Uppark, South Harting (NT)
Late seventeenth-century house having associations with Lady Hamilton and H. G. Wells. Most of the furnishings date from about 1750.

Grammar School was founded by a quilt maker named Gilbert Hannan in 1672. Famous old boys include H. G. Wells, Richard Cobden and Sir Charles Lyall, the geologist.

The curfew still tolls in Midhurst. Every night at eight the chimes ring out, it is said to commemorate a benighted traveller saved by the bell. In his gratitude, he endowed the ringing in perpetuity.

A market town from Saxon times, Midhurst was, if not rotten, certainly a borough well on the turn. In the year 1311, Edward II called on the town to send two representatives to Parliament. The right of election was vested in certain tenures of the Lords of the Borough, whether or not the tenants were residents. Some of the properties with a vote were demolished by one of the Montagues to make room for a wall around his park, but the resourceful Viscount preserved the votes with a stone inscribed 'A Burgage'. It was said that there were so few voters in Midhurst that these stones elected the Members of Parliament. The burgage tenures were sold by the trustees of the last Viscount Montague for a sum said to be 40,000 guineas, which must lead to speculation about how much Members made from being in Parliament. Cobden received £120,000 from public subscription after his Corn Laws campaign.

Cowdray was built by Shakespeare's patron, the Earl of Southampton, in about 1530. On the remarriage of the earl's mother, it passed to Sir Anthony Browne, afterwards Viscount Montague, who had received Battle Abbey from Henry VIII. Magnificent in its time, it was destroyed by fire in 1793, partly because no-one could find the key to the shed where the fire appliance was kept. Battle Abbey's great scroll was also destroyed. Tradition states that the last monk to leave Battle Abbey cursed Sir Anthony, and said that his family would perish by fire and water. Shortly after the fire at Cowdray, Viscount Montague was drowned in Switzerland, and his two

Cowdray Castle

nephews were drowned at Bognor: the curse had taken 255 years to effect. Today Cowdray is known for polo and both Prince Charles and the Duke of Edinburgh have played there on many occasions. The memorials to the Montague family are in the church of St Mary at Easebourne.

North of the village of Lurgashall is Black Down, at 919ft, the highest point

in Sussex. Tennyson lived here at Aldworth House, and wrote:

Green Sussex fading into blue,
With one grey glimpse of sea.'

Lurgashall has a very pretty village green and a church remarkable for having a sort of wooden cloister, or external gallery on the south of the nave. It is sixteenth century, and was erected

Petworth House

123

Interior, Petworth House

---

for the convenience of parishioners from
outlying parts to either eat in or shelter
in when not attending services.

Petworth is an ancient town of narrow
lanes, where the wall of the park funnels
the traffic along the A272. It was a
manor in 1042, and by the time of the
Conquest, or at least at the time of the
Domesday survey, it possessed a church,
a mill, a manor house, and pannage for
eighty hogs. Over the years, the manor
has been in the ownership of the Percys,
the Somersets, and the Wyndhams.

Petworth has a number of interesting
buildings built in the sixteenth and
seventeenth centuries. The old
almshouses, Somerset Hospital and
Somerset Lodge, are seventeenth
century, and Tudor House opposite the
church was built in 1629. New Grove
Lane, was for a time the home of
Grinling Gibbons. The pride of
Petworth however, is Petworth House,
standing in a deer park of over seven
hundred acres. The chapel dates from
1340, but the main building is Stuart. It
was built by Charles Seymour, Sixth
Duke of Somerset, in 1688-96.

One of the state rooms is known as the
Grinling Gibbons room, where the
famous wood-carver wrought birds,
flowers, fruits, and musical instruments.
There are many priceless pictures,
including a number by Turner who had
a studio in the house. The Third Earl,
George O'Brien Wyndham, was a
considerable patron of the arts, and
made Petworth House into a treasure
house. In 1795 he commissioned
Romney to paint his mistress and
children, and during the next forty years,
no fewer than 66 notable artists had
contributed 263 paintings to his
galleries. Sir Joshua Reynolds, Turner,
Van Dyck, Lely, Murillo, Hobbema,
Holbein, Velasquez, and Hogarth are all
represented in a list that reads like a
history of art. The gardens were created

by Capability Brown, and contain the finest example of an ice-house in Sussex. The grounds also contain a sculpture known as 'Alcibiades' Dog'. The dog in fact belonged to Earl Egremont, and the sculpture was commissioned from John Carew in 1829. At the north west end of the park, The Monument, is another of those once fashionable 'prospect towers', this one offering a better view than most.

The house is more like a palace, and is now owned and maintained by the National Trust. It also contains sculpture and sumptuous furniture and artefacts; china, Chippendale mirrors, and the Paul Storr Silver. The Greek sculpture in the Beauty Room is the famous Leconfield Aphrodite, from the fourth century BC. It is said that this sculpture is the work of Praxiteles.

William Cobbert, famous for his *Rural Rides*, lived in the town; and Edward Jenner is said to have performed two thousand vaccinations during a single day there.

Just south of Petworth where the A285 crosses the Western Rother at Coultershaw Bridge, there is an interesting industrial relic. The Coultershaw waterwheel and beam pump was installed by Lord Egremont in 1782, to pump water from the river to Petworth House and the town. There is also an exhibition of pumps, water supply, and the natural history of the area. There is a working watermill close by. Burton Mill was built in the eighteenth century, and is now driven by a water turbine to produce stone-ground wholemeal flour, bran, and breakfast cereal. There is a nature trail around the millpond, and through woodland, and one may fish in Burton Pond.

North of Petworth is the small village of Ebernoe, which stages the famous Horn Fair every year on 25 July. A sheep is roasted in the open air, and the head and horns are presented to the highest scorer in the associated cricket match. This custom is said to be at least five hundred years old, and carries even older pagan overtones.

It is interesting that Kirdford and the surrounding area has for long been an apple-growing area, and when it rains on St Swithin's Day (15 July) it is said that 'St Swithin is christening the apples'. Ebernoe Horn Fair would, before the introduction of the Gregorian Calendar in 1752, have been on 15 July, and so there seems to be strong evidence of a pagan fertility ceremony, later made Christian, at this time of year, possibly always connected with apples. Kirdford is known to have had a glass furnace in 1380, and in the fourteenth and fifteenth centuries this area, up to Chiddingfold in Surrey, was the centre of the English glass industry. Glass from Kirdford was

Petworth

Horsham

probably supplied for Winchester College and New College, Oxford, as well as Winchester Cathedral. There appeared to have been some specialisation in ruby glass, and to a lesser extent, blue. Set into the vicarage wall is an inscribed stone which is well worth looking out for. It is a wholehearted attack on drunkeness and the evils of alcohol, which some say was put up by the parishioners and meant for the vicar.

Billingshurst either gets its name from the Saxon *Billings,* or from the Roman engineer Belinus, who built Stane Street.

The balance of probability lies with Belinus, because Stane Street entered London at Billingsgate far away from the Saxon settlement. He would probably have been amused to know that the stretch of his work that passes through Billingshurst eventually became known as the 'Devils Road', because of its 'unnatural' straightness.

The church was enlarged and restored in 1866, but some traces of its Early English character remain. There is a very fine fifteenth-century wagon roof with 125 carved bosses. The west tower, which is twelfth century, has clasping

Warnham War Museum

buttresses and a heavy broach spire, and the porch, dating from around 1600, is of brick and timber with a bargeboard. Ye Olde Six Bells is a timber-framed, jettied building, dating from the sixteenth century, with a roof of Horsham stone slabs. The Unitarian Church is one of the best non-conformist chapels in England, having been built by William Evershed in 1754. It stands in the High Street, and looks more like a Georgian cottage. It is interesting to note that concurrent with the building of this Chapel was the widespread practice of wife-selling.

Horsham has been spelt in that way from at least 947, when it was mentioned in a Saxon charter, and the name is more likely to mean the home of horses than the home of Horsa the Saxon chief. Oddly, it does not appear in the Domesday Book, but it was given to William de Braose after the Conquest.

Two Members were sent to Parliament from 1295, and in 1617 Horsham became a Corporate Borough with a Common Seal and elected Bailiffs. The Assizes and Quarter Sessions commenced in 1307, and were held at the Town Hall or Market House as it was then known. The last Assize was held in 1830, after which the journey to Australia or the scaffold for those found guilty commenced at Lewes. A charter for an Annual Fair was granted to Horsham by Henry III in 1233. At first, the fairs were mainly concerned with corn and poultry, but in 1705 Queen Anne granted a charter for a monthly market to trade in cattle and other commodities.

The old centre of Horsham was the Carfax, a word meaning a crossroads. Ye King's Head is dated 1401, and undoubtedly at one time catered for pilgrims on their way to the shrine of St

Richard at Chichester. Horsham's most interesting street is the Causeway, which leads to the parish church of St Mary. Horsham Museum is in this street, occupying Causeway House, a lovely half-timbered building of late Tudor origin, with unusual semi-circular windows in its two gables. Numbers eleven and twelve are originally one house built in 1500, and the Manor House is a three-storey building erected in 1704.

St Mary's Church was founded in 1231 and suffered some heavy-handed restoration in 1864-5. The spire of the fifteenth-century vestry is known as the Lollards Tower, and is shingled with tiles of wood.

Horsham was once a centre for the making of horse-shoes, cross-bows, and quarrels, all of which were used on many battlefields during the Hundred Years' War.

Warnham, just north of Horsham, contains reminders of much more recent hostilities, as the Warnham War Museum is the largest private collection of World War II material in Britain. Two recent additions are a Sherman tank and a German 88mm 'tankbuster'

Crawley Shopping Centre

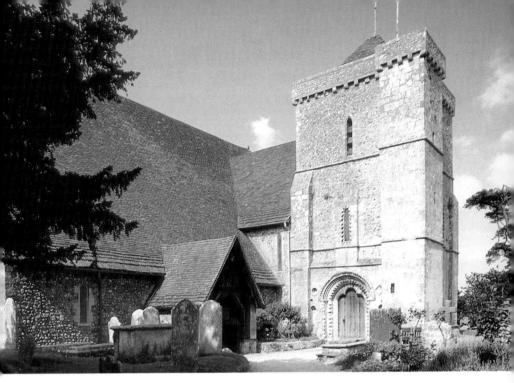

St Nicholas, Arundel

Arundel Castle

Stopham Bridge

Bosham

Ardingly Reservoir
Boating, fishing, picnic areas, nature
trails and marvellous views within a
short distance of the South of
England showground.

Priest House, West Hoathly
Fifteenth-century timber-framed
wealden hall house containing a folk
museum.

Legh Manor, Haywards Heath
Early sixteenth-century wealden
house with gardens by Gertrude
Jekyll.

Leonardslee, Horsham
Famous spring flowering garden also
famed for its autumn tints. The
rhododendrons and azaleas are
profuse and breathtaking.

Blue Idol, Coolham
An ancient building used for worship
by the Quaker, William Penn.

Cowfold Church
Contains a 10ft brass of 1433 to Prior
Neland.

Nymans, Handcross (NT)
Large, partly walled gardens with
outstanding collection of rare trees.

Wakehurst Place, Ardingly
Garden with a series of lakes and
ponds, with rare shrubs, plants, and
trees.

Warnham War Museum, Horsham
Largest private collection of militaria
in the country.

Worth Church, Horsham
A complete, unaltered Saxon church.

gun obtained from the Spanish Army;
both now facing each other in peace.

At Broadbridge Heath, Field Place is
the birthplace of the poet Shelley who as
a boy sailed his toy boats on the pond at
Warnham. Not far away is St Leonard's
Forest, a 12,000 acre tract where iron
has been extracted since Roman times.
Here it is said that a smuggler, Mick
Mills raced the Devil, and an avenue
bears his name to this day. A dragon
once dwelt in the forest, killed by St
Leonard, a French hermit of the sixth
century, while Squire Powlett, a headless
phantom, lies in wait for travellers
across the forest.

Crawley was once a quiet village with
an inn, a church, and some nice old
houses. Now it is a great amorphous
mass, steadily engulfing everything
around it.

In contrast, Lower Beeding means
Leonardslee, and Leonardslee means
breathtaking colours and gorgeous
walks. It is one of the great woodland
gardens created by the Loder family. It
occupies over a hundred acres, with
woodland walks, and hammer ponds
converted into ornamental lakes.
Although it is principally known for
rhododendrons and azaleas, there are
rare conifers, redwoods, wellingtonias, a
tulip tree, scarlet oaks, cherries,
magnolias, and a japanese birch.
Although many beautiful and rare
camellias are unfortunately now being
removed, some are being preserved in a
large garden at St Leonards-on-Sea,
where the public will have a chance to
see them. Leonardslee opens in May and
early June, and again in October for the
autumn colours which compare with
New England in the fall.

Further Information

ABBREVIATIONS:

DoE	Department of the Environment
ESDC	East Sussex District Council
FC	Forestry Commission
NCC	Nature Conservation Council
NT	National Trust
STNC	Sussex Trust for Nature Conservation
SWA	Southern Water Authority
WSCC	West Sussex County Council
SAS	Sussex Archaeological Society

BUILDINGS OPEN TO THE PUBLIC

Alfriston Clergy House (NT)
Tel: Alfriston 870001
Open: April-October, daily 11am-6pm or sunset. Last admission half an hour before closing.
Fourteenth-century thatched priest's house. Shop.

Arundel Castle
Tel: Arundel 882297
Open:April-October, daily (except Saturday) 1-6pm, July-August and all Bank Holidays daily (except Saturday) 12 noon-5pm. Last admission 4pm.
Family seat of the Dukes of Norfolk. Shop.

Batemans (NT)
Burwash
Tel: Burwash 882302
Open: April-October, Saturday to Wednesday 11am-6pm and Good Friday.
Seventeenth-century ironmasters house. Home of Rudyard Kipling. Shop and tearoom.

Battle Abbey
Tel: Battle 3792
Open: all year, DoE standard hours.
Site of the famous Battle of 1066.

Blue Idol
Horsham
Tel: Coolham 241
Open: daily.
Ancient building used by William Penn. Refreshments on Sundays.

Bodiam Castle (NT)
Bodiam
Tel: Staplecross 436
Open: April-October, 10am-6pm or sunset; November-March, 10am-to sunset. Last entry half an hour before closing.
Fairy-tale castle in a moat. Shop and tearoom.

Bridge Cottage
Uckfield
Tel: Uckfield 4841 or 2969
Open: all year, Saturday 10am-4pm.
A timber-framed Wealden Hall House, from about 1400.

Danny
Hassocks
Tel: Hurstpierpoint 833000
Open: May-September, Wednesday and Thursday 2-5pm.
Elizabethan 'E' shaped house, about 1595.

Firle Place

Firle
Tel: Glynde 335
Open: June-September, Sunday,
Monday and Wednesday 2.15-5pm also
Thursdays in August. Bank Holiday
Sunday and Monday, same hours.
Tudor and Georgian house, home of the
Gage family for 500 years. Shop and
tearoom.

Glynde Place

Tel: Glynde 337
Open: June-September, Wednesday and
Thursday 2.15-5.30pm. Easter Sunday
and Monday, plus Bank Holiday
Monday, same hours.
Sixteenth-century house containing
many treasures. Tearoom.

Goodwood House

Chichester
Tel: Chichester 774107
Open: May-October, Sunday and
Monday; August, Tuesday and
Thursday 2-5pm.
Home of the Dukes of Richmond and
Gordon. Superb paintings and furniture.
Shop and tearoom.

Great Dixter

Northiam
Tel: Northiam 3160
Open: daily April-mid-October (except
Monday), 2-5pm. Also remaining
weekends in October and Bank Holiday
Monday, same hours.
Fifteenth-century timbered house with
notable garden.

Haremere Hall

Etchingham
Tel: Etchingham 501
Open: daily April-November (except
Monday), 10.30am-5pm. Also Bank
Holiday Monday. Horses presented and
demonstrated at 11am and 3pm.
Seventeenth-century manor house plus
working heavy horses.

Hastings Castle

Tel: Hastings 424242
Open: April-September, 10am-5pm.
Remains of William the Conqueror's
first English castle. Refreshments
nearby.

Herstmonceux Castle

Herstmonceux
Tel: Eastbourne 833171
Open: Easter-September, Monday-
Friday, grounds 12 noon-5.30pm,
exhibition 2-5.30pm. Saturday, Sunday
and public holidays 10.30am-5.30pm.
Home of the Royal Greenwich
Observatory. Only two rooms open.
Cafeteria.

Lamb House (NT)

Rye
Tel: Rye 223763
Open: April to October, Wednesday and
Saturday 2-6pm. Last entry 5.30pm.
Home of Henry James and E. F.
Benson.

Lewes Castle (SAS)

Tel: Lewes 4379
Open: all year weekdays, 10am-5pm or
dusk; April-October, Sunday 11am-
5.30pm.
Keep of William de Warrenes' castle
with extensive views.

Michelham Priory (SAS)

Upper Dicker
Tel: Hailsham 844224
Open: April-October, daily 11am-
5.30pm.
Augustinian Priory founded 1229 with a
working water-mill. Restaurant.

Monks House (NT)

Rodmell
Tel: Lewes 2385
Open: April-October, Wednesday and
Saturday 2-6pm.
Home of Leonard and Virginia Woolf.

Newtimber Place
Hassocks
Tel: Hurstpierpoint 833104
Open: May-August, Thursday 2-5pm.
Moated seventeenth-century house with
dovecote.

Old Mint House
Pevensey
Tel: Eastbourne 762337
Open: all year, Monday-Saturday 9am-
5pm. Closed Bank Holidays.
Fourteenth-century former home of
Andrew Borde. Now an antique
showroom.

Petworth House (NT)
Tel: Petworth 42207
Open: April-October, daily (excluding
Monday, Friday and Tuesdays after
Bank Holidays) 2-6pm. Bank Holiday
Monday 2-6pm. Last admission 5.30pm.
Seventeenth-century house with
outstanding picture collection. Shop and
tearoom.

Pevensey Castle (DoE)
Pevensey
Tel: Eastbourne 762604
Open: DoE standard hours.
Norman Keep within a Roman fort.
Shop.

Preston Manor
Brighton
Tel: Brighton 603005
Open: all year, Wednesday-Saturday
10am-5pm, Sunday 2-5pm. Closed
Good Friday, Christmas and New Year.
Fine collection of furniture, silver, glass
and china.

Priest House (SAS)
West Hoathly
Tel: Sharpthorne 810479
Open: April-September, daily (except
Friday) 11am-5pm, Sunday 2-5pm.
Fifteenth-century timber-framed house
with folk museum.

Royal Pavilion
Brighton
Tel: Brighton 603005
Open: June-September, daily 10am-
6.30pm; October-June, daily 10am-5pm.
Nash's extravaganza built for the Prince
Regent. Tea-room and shop.

Sackville College
East Grinstead
Tel: East Grinstead 25436
Open: May-October, daily 2-5pm.
Jacobean almshouse.

St Mary's Hospital
Chichester
Tel: Chichester 783377
Open: daily (except Sunday and
Monday) April-October, 2-5pm;
October-April 11am-12 noon and
2-4pm.
Thirteenth-century almshouse.

Sheffield Park
Uckfield
Tel: Danehill 790531
Open: May-October, Wednesday,
Thursday and Sunday 2-5pm. Also
Easter Sunday and Monday.
Tudor house remodelled by James
Wyatt.

Standen (NT)
East Grinstead
Tel: East Grinstead 23029
Open: April-October, Wednesday,
Thursday, Saturday and Sunday
2-5.30pm. Last entry 5pm.
A large house designed by Philip Webb.
Shop and tea-room.

Uppark (NT)
South Harting
Tel: Harting 317
Open: April-September, Wednesday,
Thursday, Sunday and Bank Holiday
Monday 2-6pm.
Notable mansion of 1690 with
furnishings mainly about 1750. Shop
and tea-room.

Beeches Farm
Uckfield
Tel: Uckfield 2391
Open: all year, daily 10am-5pm or dusk.
Lawns, borders, roses, yew trees, and a
sunken garden.

Borde Hill
Haywards Heath
Tel: Haywards Heath 450326
Open: April-September, Wednesday,
Thursday, Saturday, Sunday and Bank
Holidays 10am-6pm; March-October,
Saturday and Sunday 10am-6pm.
Large garden with camellias, magnolias,
azaleas, rhododendrons, rare trees, and
woodland.

Brickwall
Northiam
Tel: Northiam 2492
Open: April-mid-July, Wednesday,
Saturday 2-4pm.
Eighteenth-century bowling alley and
sunken topiary garden.

Charleston Manor
West Dean
Tel: Eastbourne 870267
Open: April-November, daily 11am-
6pm.
Typical old English garden.

Cobblers Garden
Jarvis Brook
Tel: Crowborough 5969
Open: May, June, July and August,
some Sundays 2.30-6pm.
Shrubs, herbaceous borders, and a water
garden.

Denmans
Fontwell
Tel: Eastergate 2313
Open: late March-October, Saturday
and Sunday 2-6pm.
Walled gardens, shrubs, climbers, and a
gravel garden.

Great Dixter
Northiam
Tel: Northiam 3160
Open: April-mid-October, daily
(excluding Monday) 2-5pm. Also Bank
Holiday Monday, and weekends latter
half of October; July to August, Sunday
11am-5pm.
Famous garden designed by Sir Edwin
Lutyens, and Christopher Lloyd.

Herstmonceux Castle
Herstmonceux
Tel: Eastbourne 833171
Open: Good Friday-October, Monday
to Friday 12 noon-5.30pm, Saturday,
Sunday and public holidays 10.30am-
5.30pm.
200-acre grounds include rose garden,
herbaceous borders and woods.

Highdown Gardens
Goring-by-Sea
Tel: Worthing 501054
Open: all year, Monday-Friday 10am-
4.30pm; April-September, Saturday,
Sunday and Bank Holidays 10am-8pm.
A five-acre chalk garden.

Holly Gate Cactus Nursery
Ashington
Tel: Ashington 892930
Open: all year (except Christmas), 9am-
5pm.
Unique collection of over 20,000 cacti
and succulents.

Horsted Place Gardens
Uckfield
Tel: Brighton 681486
Open: May-October, Sunday,
Wednesday, Thursday and public
holidays, also Easter Sunday and
Monday 2-6pm.
Beautiful Victorian garden.

Kidbrooke Park
Forest Row
Tel: Forest Row 2275
Open: August, daily 9am-5pm.
Parkland with wild garden, bog garden,
ha-ha, and pergola.

Legh Manor
Ansty
Tel: Haywards Heath 413428
Open: April-October, second and third
Wednesday and second Saturday each
month 2.30-5.30pm.
Five-acre garden designed by G. Jekyll.

Leonardslee
Lower Beeding
Tel: Lower Beeding 212 or 305
Open: April-mid-June, daily 10am-
6pm. October, Saturday and Sunday
10am-6pm.
Extensive gardens with lakes, famous for
camellias and rhododendrons.

Michelham Priory
Upper Dicker
Tel: Hailsham 844224
Open: Easter-October, daily 11am-
5.30pm.
Six acres of gardens in beautiful
surroundings.

Newick Park
Tel: Newick 2915
Open: March-November, Friday-
Monday 2-5.30pm.
Eighteenth-century park with two
gardens and farmland walk.

Nymans Garden (NT)
Handcross
Tel: Bookham 53401
Open: April-November, daily (except
Monday and Friday), also Bank Holiday
Monday 11am-6pm or sunset.
Outstanding garden with attractions.

Parham Park
Pulborough
Tel: Storrington 2866
Open: Easter Sunday-last Sunday in
September. House, Sunday and Bank
Holidays, 2-6pm. Garden, Wednesday,
Thursday, Sunday and Bank Holidays,
plus Saturday in July and August,
1-6pm.

Sheffield Park (NT)
Fletching
Tel: Danehill 790655
Open: April-mid-November, Tuesday-
Saturday 11am-6pm. Sunday and Bank
Holiday Monday 2-6pm.
Wonderful garden by Capability Brown
with five lakes.

Standen (NT)
East Grinstead
Tel: East Grinstead 23029
Open: April-November, Wednesday,
Thursday, Saturday and Sunday 2-6pm.
Hillside garden with superb views.

Wakehurst Place (NT)
Ardingly
Tel: Haywards Heath 892701
Open: January, November, December,
daily 10am-4pm; February, March, daily
10am-5pm; April-September, daily
10am-7pm.
Exotic plants, managed by Royal
Botanic Gardens, Kew.

West Dean Gardens
West Dean
Tel: Singleton 301
Open: April-October, daily 10am-6pm.
Last admission 5pm.
35-acre informal garden, partly by
Gertrude Jekyll.

MUSEUMS

Listed alphabetically by town.

Chalk Pits Museum
BR Station Yard, Amberley.
Tel: Bury 370
Open: April-October, Wednesday-
Sunday and Bank Holidays 11am-5pm.
Industrial Archaeology.

Arundel Museum
Heritage Centre, 61 High Street.
Tel: Arundel 882726
Open: Easter-October, Tuesday-
Saturday 10.30am-12.30pm and 2-5pm,
Sunday 2-5pm.

Toy and Military Museum
23 High Street, Arundel.
Tel: Arundel 883101 or 882908
Open: all year, Saturday, Sunday; June-August, daily 10.30am-5.30pm.

Museum of Curiosities
6 High Street, Arundel.
Tel: Arundel 882420
Open: April-October, daily 10.30am-1pm and 2.15-5.30pm; October, daily 2.15-5pm.
Stuffed tableaux and strange objects.

Battle Museum
Langton House, High Street.
Tel: Battle 3899 (Curator)
Open: Easter-October, Monday-Saturday 10am-1pm and 2-5pm, Sunday 2.30-5.30pm.
Local history, and events of 1066.

Bexhill Museum
Egerton Road.
Tel: Bexhill 215361
Open: April-October, Monday, Thursday, Saturday 10am-4pm; June, July, August, Sunday 2.30-4pm; November-March, Monday, Thursday, Saturday 10am-1pm.
Local geology, archaeology, and natural history.

Manor Costume Museum
Manor Gardens, Bexhill.
Tel: Bexhill 215361
Open: Easter-October, Tuesday-Friday 10.30am-1pm and 2.30-5.30pm, Saturday, Sunday and Bank Holidays 2.30-5.30pm.
Period costumes, dolls, lace and toys.

House of Pipes
Bramber.
Tel: Steyning 812122
Open: all year, daily 9am-6pm.
50,000 exhibits from 180 countries, a 'smokiana'.

Booth Museum of Natural History
194 Dyke Road, Brighton.
Tel: Brighton 552586 or 603005
Open: all year Monday-Saturday (except Thursday), 10am-5pm. Sunday 2-5pm.

Brighton Museum and Art Gallery
Church Street.
Tel: Brighton 603005
Open: all year, Tuesday-Saturday 10am-5.45pm, Sunday 2-5pm.
Art, Ethnography, Ceramics, Archaeology, and Fashion.

The British Engineerium
Nevill Road, Hove.
Tel: Brighton 559583
Open: all year, daily 10am-5.30pm.
Steam engines and engineering.

The Barlow Collection
University of Sussex Library, Falmer, Brighton.
Tel: Brighton 606755
Open: during term, Tuesday and Thursday 11.30am-2.30pm.
3,000 years of Chinese civilisation.

Stanmer Rural Museum
Stanmer Village, Brighton.
Tel: Brighton 603005
Open: Easter-November, Thursday 11am-1pm and 2.30-5pm, Sunday 2.30-5pm.
Agricultural exhibits.

National Museum of Penny Slot Machines
Palace Pier, Brighton.
Tel: Brighton 608620
Open: April-November, daily 11am to one hour before dusk.

Chichester District Museum
29 Little London.
Tel: Chichester 784683
Open: all year, Tuesday-Saturday 10am-5.30pm.
Local history, geology and social history, plus Royal Sussex Regiment Collection.

Guildhall Museum
Priory Park, North Street, Chichester.
Tel: Chichester 784683
Open: June-September, Tuesday-
Saturday 1-5pm.
Local archaeology.

Pallant House Gallery
9 North Pallant, Chichester.
Tel: Chichester 774557
Open: all year, Tuesday-Saturday 10am-
5.30pm.
Porcelain, paintings and sculpture.

The Redoubt Fortress
Royal Parade, Eastbourne.
Tel: Eastbourne 33952
Open: Easter-November, daily 10am-
5.30pm.
Coastguard, Cinque Port and Sussex
Combined Services Museum.

Tower 73
King Edwards Parade, Eastbourne.
Tel: Eastbourne 35809
Open: Easter-mid-November, daily
9.30am-5.30pm.
History of area and Martello towers.

The Lifeboat Museum
Grand Parade, Eastbourne.
Tel: Eastbourne 27474
Open: Easter-Christmas, daily 9.30am-
1pm and 1.30-4pm.

**Towner Art Gallery and Local History
Museum**
Manor Gardens, High Street, Old Town,
Eastbourne.
Tel: Eastbourne 21635 or 25112
Open: all year Monday- Saturday 10am-
5pm, Sunday 2-5pm. Closed Good
Friday and winter Mondays.
Local history and specialised art
collections.

Town Museum
East Court, East Grinstead.
Tel: East Grinstead 25005
Open: all year, Monday 2-4pm,
Saturday 2-5pm.

Hailsham Museum
Western Road.
Tel: Hailsham 840604 (Tourist
Information Centre)
Open: May- September, Wednesday
10.30am-1pm. Also two weeks at Easter.
Local history, domestic and agricultural
implements.

Hastings Museum and Art Gallery
Cambridge Road.
Tel: Hastings 435952
Open: all year Monday-Saturday 10am-
1pm and 2-5pm, Sunday 3-5pm.
Wealden iron, Sussex pottery, local
history and Asiatic display.

Hastings Museum of Local History
High Street.
Tel: Hastings 425855
Open: Easter-October, Monday-
Saturday 10am-1pm and 2-5pm;
October-Easter 2-5pm.
Local, Norman and Cinque Ports
history.

Fisherman's Museum
Rock-a-Nore, Hastings.
Tel: Hastings 424242 (Tourist
Information Centre)
Open: Easter-October, Saturday-
Thursday 10am-12 noon and 2-5pm.
History of local fishing industry.

Museum of Music, Mirth and Amusement
Hastings Pier.
Tel: Hastings 422566
Open: all year, weekends 10am-5pm.

Henfield Museum
New Village Hall, Henfield.
Open: all year, Tuesday, Thursday and
Saturday 10am-12 noon, Wednesday
2.30-4.30pm.

Horsham Museum
9 The Causeway.
Tel: Horsham 54959
Open: all year, Tuesday-Friday, 1-5pm,
Saturday 10am-5pm.
Local history, crafts, rural life and a folk
museum.

Hove Museum of Art
19 New Church Road, Hove.
Tel: Brighton 779410
Open: all year, Tuesday-Friday 10am-1pm and 2-5pm, Saturday 10am-1pm and 2-4.30pm.
Paintings, miniatures, pottery, glass, and silver.

Military Heritage Museum
1 Albion Street, Lewes.
Tel: Lewes 3137
Open: April-October, 10am-1pm and 2-5pm.
British Army 1660-1914.

Museum of Local History
Anne of Cleves House, Southover High Street, Lewes.
Tel: Lewes 4610
Open: mid-February - mid-November, Sunday 2-5pm.
Wealden iron and folk museum.

Museum of Sussex Archaeology
Barbican House, High Street, Lewes.
Tel: Lewes 4379
Open: all year, Monday-Saturday 10am-5.30pm; April-October, Sunday 2-5.30pm.

Littlehampton Museum
12A River Road.
Tel: Littlehampton 5149
Open: April-October, Tuesday-Saturday; November-April, Thursday-Saturday 10.30am-1pm and 2-4pm.
Local history with maritime flavour.

Midhurst Museum
Cowdray Park.
Tel: Midhurst 2215
Open: April-October, Friday-Tuesday 10am-5.30pm.
Engravings, paintings, furniture, books, etc, in one wing of ruins.

Perigoe Workshop Museum
Oak House, Northiam.
Tel: Northiam 3215
Open: April-October, daily (except Monday) 2-5pm.
Builder's and carpenter's workshop.

Buckleys Shop Museum
14 High Street, Polegate.
Tel: Polegate 2100
Open: all year, Monday-Saturday, 10am-5.30pm, Sunday 2.30-5.30pm.
Arcade of Victorian and Edwardian shops, plus traditional tea-room.

Milling Museum
Polegate Windmill, Park Croft, Polegate.
Tel: Eastbourne 54845
Open: Easter-October, Sunday 2.30-5.30pm.

Robertsbridge Aeronautical Museum
Bush Barn, Robertsbridge.
Tel: Tunbridge Wells 890386
Open: all year, last Sunday in month 2.30-5.30pm; May-September, Tuesday 7.30-9pm.
Salvaged parts of war planes.

Rottingdean Grange Museum and Art Gallery
The Green, Rottingdean.
Tel: Brighton 31004
Open: all year, Monday, Thursday and Saturday 10am-5pm, Tuesday and Friday 10am-1pm and 2-5pm, Sunday 2-5pm. Closed Good Friday.
Part of National Toy Collection, Kipling mementoes and art.

Rye Museum
Ypres Tower, Gun Garden.
Tel: Rye 223254
Open: Easter- mid-October, Monday-Saturday 10.30am-1pm and 2.15-5.30pm, Sunday 11.30am-1pm and 2.15-5.30pm.
Local and Cinque Ports history in thirteenth-century tower.

Cherries Folk Museum
Playden, Rye.
Tel: Rye 223224
Open: any reasonable time by appointment.
Country life before 1946.

Nortons Farm Museum
Sedlescombe.
Tel: Sedlescombe 471
Open: May-September, daily 9am-5pm.
Agricultural Museum on A21 at Kent
Street.

Marlipins Museum
High Street, Shoreham.
Tel: Shoreham 62994
Open: May-October, MondaySaturday
10am-1pm and 2-5pm, Sunday 2-5pm.
Local history in twelfth-century
building.

Weald and Downland Open Air Museum
Singleton, Chichester.
Tel: Singleton 348
Open: April and May, daily (except
Monday); June, July, August, daily
11am-5pm; November-April, Sunday
and Wednesday 11am-4pm. Bank
Holidays 11am-5pm.
Many interesting buildings, saved and
re-erected here.

Tangmere Museum of Military Aviation
Tangmere Aerodrome, Chichester.
Tel: Chichester 775223
Open: March-November, daily 11am-
5.30pm.
Aviation exhibits on famous Battle of
Britain airfield.

Warnham War Museum
Durfold Hill, Warnham, Nr Horsham.
Tel: Horsham 65607
Open: Easter-October, daily 10am-4pm.
November-Easter, daily 10am-4pm.
Largest private collection of World War
II vehicles and militaria.

Wilmington Priory Museum
The Street, Wilmington, nr Polegate (off
A27).
Tel: Eastbourne 870537
Open: mid-March-mid-October,
Monday-Saturday (except Tuesday)
11am-5pm, Sunday 2-5pm.
Agricultural museum in thirteenth-
century priory.

Court Hall Museum
Winchelsea, nr Rye.
Open: May-September, weekdays
10.30am-12.30pm and 2.30-5.30pm,
Sunday 2.30-5.30pm.
Local and Cinque Ports history in
fourteenth-century prison, opposite the
church.

Museum of Sussex Folklore
Parsonage Row Cottages, High Street,
Tarring, Worthing.
Tel: Worthing 36385
Open: March-mid-December, Tuesday-
Saturday 2.15-5pm.
Sussex folklore and customs.

Worthing Museum and Art Gallery
Chapel Road.
Tel: Worthing 39999
Open: April-October, Monday-Saturday
11am-6pm; November-April, Monday-
Saturday 10am-5pm.
Local history, archaeology, costumes,
toys and downland.

CHURCHES OF SPECIAL INTEREST

Battle
Medieval painting and brasses.

Bosham
Saxon on Roman foundation. Burial
place of Canute's daughter.

Bishopstone
Saxon church with Saxon sundial.

Boxgrove
Famous De La Warr tomb-chapel.

Chichester
Cathedral commenced in 1091, with a
campanile.

Climping
Reputed to be the most perfect church in
West Sussex.

Cowfold
10ft-long brass of 1433 to Prior Nelond.

Etchingham
Four fine de Etchyngham brasses.

Hardham
Noted for murals.

Rye
'Cathedral of East Sussex'. Oldest
turret clock in England with famous
quarter boys.

Sompting
Saxon with unique Rhenish Helm.

Trotton
Oldest brass in England of a woman,
Lady Margaret Camoys 1310.

Wadhurst
Unique collection of cast-iron grave
slabs.

Winchelsea
Perfect Decorated church with famous
Alard tombs.

Worth
Complete unaltered Saxon church.

ZOOS AND WILDLIFE PARKS

Drusillas Zoo
Alfriston, 4 miles north of Seaford off
the A27.
Tel: (0323) 870234
Open: all year, daily 10am-6pm.
Ideal childrens' zoo, specialising in
cuddly animals. Restaurant and shops.

Wildfowl Trust
Mill Road, ½ mile north of Arundel.
Tel: (0903) 883355
Open: April-November, daily 9.30am-
6.30pm; November-April, daily 9.30am-
5pm.
55 acres of lakes and water meadows
with observatory and hides. Birds from
all over the world, many rare, plus many
native visitors.

Zootopia
Rainbows End, Hotham Park, Bognor.
Tel: (0243) 824858
Open: all year, daily 10am-dusk.
Zoo combined with 'World of Fantasy'.
Shop and cafeteria.

Aquarium and Dolphinarium
Marine Parade, Brighton.
Tel: (0273) 604233
Open: all year, daily (summer) 9am-
6.30pm, (winter) 9.30am-5pm.
Thousands of marine tropical and
freshwater fish, sea-lions, seals, turtles,
plus the amazing dolphins. Cafeteria
and shop.

The Butterfly Centre
Royal Parade, Eastbourne.
Tel: (0323) 645522
Open: Easter-November, daily 10am-
5.30pm.
Tropical, semi-tropical and native
butterflies flying free over landscaped
gardens with fountains, waterfalls and
pools. Shop.

Spring Hill Wildfowl Park
Forest Row, 3 miles south of East
Grinstead.
Tel: (034282) 2783
Open: all year, daily 10am-dusk.
Around 1,000 species from all over the
world in 10 acres of grounds. Shop and
cafeteria.

Bentley Wildfowl Park
Halland, 7 miles north-east of Lewes off
the B2192.
Tel: (082584) 573
Open: Easter-October, daily 11am-
4.30pm. Winter weekends (except
December) 11am-4pm.
The Gerald Askew wildfowl collection
in beautiful grounds. There is also a
motor museum and the beautiful
Bentley House. Shop and tea-room.

Raystede Animal Welfare Centre
Ringmer, 2 miles north-east of Lewes off the B2192.
Tel: (082584) 252
Open: all year, daily 10am-1pm and 2-4pm.
Dogs, cats, donkeys, horses, rabbits, and badgers being looked after. Shop.

The Living World
3 miles east of Seaford off the A259.
Tel: (0323) 870100
Open: all year, daily 10am-5pm.
An exhibition of all types of insects, scorpions, spiders, mantids, and coastal marine life displayed in two barns at Seven Sisters Country Park. Shop.

Ashdown Forest Farm
Wych Cross, East Sussex
Tel: 082571 2040
Open: daily except Christmas Day, 10am-dusk.
Farm set in the centre of the Ashdown Forest, stocked with rare and ancient breeds of farm animals and poultry.

STEAM RAILWAYS

Bluebell Railway
Sheffield Park, nr Uckfield.
Tel: (082572) 2370
Open: all year, daily service July and August. Sheds always open.
The first preserved line which at present runs approximately 5 miles to Horsted Keynes. Almost entirely devoted to the Southern Railway, including West Country, Schools, and Brittania classes and the Reverend Awdry's famous *Stepney*. Tea-room and shop.

Kent and East Sussex Railway
Tenterden, Kent.
Tel: (05806) 2943
Open: April-Christmas, daily in summer season.
This light railway is included because it is due to run to Bodiam in the near future and will travel several miles into Sussex. Buffet and shop.

WINDMILLS AND WATERMILLS

Burwash
Batemans Water-mill (NT), $\frac{1}{2}$ mile south-west of Burwash off the A265.
Tel: (0435) 882302
Open: April-November, Saturday-Wednesday 11am-6pm.
Working mill containing the oldest water turbine in Britain, installed by Kipling to generate electricity. Sales of flour.

Chailey
Founders Mill, 6 miles south-east of Haywards Heath, at the junction of the A275 and A272.
Smock mill dating from about 1830. Viewable from the outside only, and said to stand in the centre of Sussex.

Clayton
Jack and Jill Windmills, $1\frac{1}{2}$ miles south of Hassocks off the A273.
Tel: (07918) 3297
Open: by arrangement and on some Sundays in summer.
Jack, the tower mill, was built here in 1866 while Jill, a post mill dating from 1821, was dragged here by oxen in 1851.

Cross-In-Hand
Cross-In-Hand Mill, off the A267 north of village.
Viewable from the outside only at present, this post mill — the largest in Sussex — started life at Mt Ephrain in 1806 and was moved here in 1863.

Hailsham
Michelham Priory Watermill, 7 miles north of Eastbourne off the A22.
Tel: (0323) 844224
Open: April-mid-October, daily 11am-5.30pm.
Working mill in Priory grounds, restored in 1971. Sales of flour.

Halnaker

Halnaker Mill, 5 miles north-east of Chichester off the A285.
Open: at all times.
Dating from 1740, this is the oldest tower mill in Sussex.

Henfield

Woods Mill, 1 mile south of Henfield on A2037.
Tel: (0273) 492630
Open: Easter-October, Tuesday, Thursday and Saturday 2-6pm, Sunday and holidays 11am-6pm.
Eighteenth-century water-mill serving as headquarters for the Sussex Trust for Nature Conservation, containing shop and many displays.

Hove

West Blatchington Mill, north of Hove on the A2038.
Tel: (0273) 775400
Open: May-October, Sunday and holidays 2.30-5pm.
An hexagonal smock mill standing on a barn, and dates from 1724.

Keymer

Oldlands Mill, ¾ mile north-east of Keymer.
Open: as advertised.
A post mill dating from bout 1690.

Mayfield

Argos Hill Mill, 1 mile north of Mayfield, at junction of A267 and B2101.
Viewable from the outside only, a post mill built about 1831-43. It is hoped that it will eventually open to the public.

Nutley

Nutley Mill, 1 mile north of Nutley off the A22.
Tel: (0825) 2969
Open: Easter-September, last Sunday in month, also Bank Holidays.
The oldest working windmill in Sussex, this is an open-trestle post mill dating from about 1675 and moved here in 1810.

Petworth

Burton Water-mill, 2 miles south of Petworth off the A285.
Open: Saturday pm to Wednesday 5pm.
Working mill dating from 1784. Sales of flour.

Polegate

Park Croft Mill, west of Polegate off A22.
Tel: (0323) 54845
Open: Easter-October, Sunday and Bank Holiday Monday 2.30-5.30pm.
A tower mill built in 1817 containing a milling museum.

Rottingdean

Black or Beacon Mill, on cliffs by A259.
Viewable from the outside only, a smock mill dating from 1802.

Selsey

Medmerry Mill, 1 mile off the B2145 in Mill Lane, Selsey.
Viewable from the outside, this tower mill built in 1820 is now a caravan camp shop.

Shipley

Kings or Bellocs Mill, 5 miles south of Horsham off the B2224.
Tel: (040387) 310
Open: May-October, first weekend in month, also Bank Holidays.
A smock mill built in 1879, restored as a memorial to Hilaire Belloc, now contains an exhibition devoted to him.

Stone Cross

Stone Cross Mill, Polegate, on A259 near junction of B2104.
Tel: (0323) 763277
Viewable from the outside, this tower mill built in 1876 has been restored single-handedly by the owner. It is hoped that it will soon open daily.

Worthing
High Salvington Mill, Furze Road,
Worthing.
Tel: (0903) 39999
Open: as advertised.
An unusual post mill of about 1700,
standing on a barn.

Bevis's Thumb
A long mound or barrow approximately
150ft long situated near the summit of
the Downs at North Marden, 6 miles
south-east of Petersfield.

Bignor Roman Villa
Near Pulborough.
Tel: Sutton (07989) 259
Open: June-September, daily 10am-
6pm; March and October, Tuesday -
Sunday 10am-5pm; April-May,
Tuesday-Sunday 10am-6pm.
Large villa containing extremely fine
mosaics.

Bow Hill
Disc or bell barrows situated at Kingley
Vale, near Staughton, 5 miles north-east
of Emsworth. There are other disc
barrows all along the South Downs way.

Cissbury
Iron Age hillfort with remains of
Neolithic flint mines, 1½ miles east of
Findon. Other Neolithic flint mines exist
at Harrow Hill, 2 miles went of Findon,
and at Stoke Down above Burpham.
Other Iron Age hillforts are situated at
The Caburn above Lewes, Hollingbury
north of Brighton, and Wolstonbury
near Pyecombe.

Fishbourne Roman Palace
Near Chichester.
Tel: Chichester (0243) 785859
Open: March, April and October, daily
10am-5pm; May-September, daily
10am-6pm; November, daily 10am-4pm;
December, January and February,
Sunday 10am-4pm.
Palace of vassal King Cogidubnus.
Largest Roman residence excavated in
Britain.

Barnsgate Manor
Herons Ghyll, 4 miles north of Uckfield
on A26.
Tel: (082571) 2854
Open: all year, groups by arrangement.
Tours, tasting, wine museum. 21 acres.
Restaurant.

Breaky Bottom
2 miles south-west of Rodmell, 1½ miles
off the A26, near Lewes.
Tel: (07916) 6427
Open: June-September, by arrangement.
Tasting, winery. 4 acres.

Car-Taylor
Yew Tree Farm, Westfield, 5 miles north
of Hastings on A28.
Tel: (0424) 752501
Open: May-October, Wednesday-
Sunday 10am-5pm.
Tours, tasting, museum, shop. 21 acres.
Refreshments.

Castle House
Plumpton Green, Lewes.
Tel: (0273) 890306
Tours by arrangement. Sales. 2 acres.

Chilsdown
Old Station House, Singleton, 6 miles
north of Chichester off the A286.
Tel: (024363) 398
Open: May-October, daily 10am-5pm.
Tours, tasting, shop. 13 acres.

Downers
Clappers Lane, Fulking, 3 miles south-east of Henfield off the A281.
Tel: (079156) 484
Open: June-September, Sunday 11am-7pm.
Tours, tasting, sales. 6 acres.

Flexerne
Fletching Common, Newick.
Tel: (082572) 2548
Tours by arrangement. 4 acres.

Marden Down
Bow Hill Farm, East Marden, Chichester.
Tel: (024359) 255
Tours by arrangement. 4 acres.

Merrydown Wine Company
Horam, 5 miles north of Hailsham off the A267.
Tel: (04353) 2254/2401
Open: mid-May - October, daily.
Tours, tasting, cider, shop.

Rock Lodge
Scaynes Hill, 5 miles north of Lewes on the A272.
Tel: (044486) 224
Open: July-September, Sunday 11am-4pm.
Tours, tasting, sales. 3½ acres.

St Georges
Waldron Vineyards, 3 miles south-west of Heathfield off the A267.
Tel: (04353) 2156
Open: June-September, 11am-5pm, Sunday 12 noon-5pm.
Tours, tasting, sales. 5 acres.
Refreshments and food.

Valley Wine Cellars
Alfriston, 4 miles north of Seaford on A27.
Tel: (0323) 870234/870532
Open: April-October, daily 11am-6pm.
Tours, tasting, shop, garden centre, Drusillas Zoo. 1 acre. Restaurant and tea-room.

Apuldram Manor Rose Centre
Chichester.
Open: daily 9am-6pm.
20,000 roses, with ramblers, climbers, shrubs, floribundas, and hybrid trees.
Guided tours and refreshments.

Arlington Raceway
Near Hailsham.
Tel: (0323) 841642 for details of events.
Open: as advertised.
Stock Car and speedway racing.

Bosham Walk
Tel: Bosham (0243) 572475
Open: daily 10am-5.30pm.
Twelve craft shops under one roof in an old Sussex street scene.

Brighton Marina
Tel: Brighton (0273) 693636
Open: daily 9am-dusk.
Large marina containing many features, including HMS *Cavalier*, a World War II destroyer.

Coombes Farm Tours
Tel: Shoreham (07917) 2028
Open: April-October, daily by arrangement.
Tours show the life of a working farm.

Fort Newhaven
Tel: Brighton (0273) 513600
Open: April-November, daily 10am-6pm; November-April, daily 10am-4pm.
Restored nineteenth-century fort, plus exhibits, crafts and exhibitions.

Hastings Embroidery
Town Hall.
Tel: Hastings (0424) 424242
Open: June-September, Monday-Saturday 10am-1pm and 2-5pm; October-May, Monday-Friday 11.30am-5.30pm.

Hastings Model Village
Tel: Hastings (0424) 427861
Open: May-mid-September, daily
10am-6pm.
Miniature Tudor village, White Rock
Gardens.

St Clements Caves
Tel: Hastings (0424) 422964
Open: April-September, daily 10.15am-
12.30pm and 1.30-5.15pm; October-
March, Saturday and Sunday 10.30am-
12.30pm and 2-5pm.
Famous smuggling caves, West Hill,
Hastings.

Sound and Light Show
Strand Quay, Rye.
Tel: Rye (0797) 223902
Open: April-November, daily 10.30am-
5pm.
Model with *son et lumiere* effects telling
the story of Rye.

Sussex County Cricket Ground
Eaton Road, Hove.
Tel: Hove (0273) 772766
Open: as advertised.
The home of Sussex cricket with first
class matches throughout the season.

Sussex Shire Horses
Haremere Hall, Etchingham.
Tel: Etchingham (058081) 501
Open: Easter-November, Tuesday-
Sunday and Bank Holidays 10.30am-
5pm. Presentations at 11am and 3pm.
Twice daily presentations of a wide
variety of heavy horse breeds. Shop and
home-made refreshments.

NATURE TRAILS, RESERVES AND COUNTRY
PARKS

===

Abbots Wood Trail (FC)
On Arlington-Hailsham road near
Friston Forest.
2 miles long.

Ardingly Reservoir Trail (SWA)
3 miles north of Haywards Heath off the
B2028.

Arlington Reservoir Trail (Eastbourne
Water Works Co)
3 miles south-west of Hailsham off the
A27.
4 miles long.

Ashdown Forest Country Park
(Conservators of Ashdown Forest)
1 mile south of Forest Row off the A22.

Barcombe Mills Nature Reserve (Mid-
Sussex Water Co)
3 miles north of Lewes, 1½ miles east of
Barcombe off the A26.

Beachy Head Country Park
4½ miles south-west of Eastbourne.

Bewl Bridge Reservoir Trail (SWA and
STNC)
Reached by B2100 and B2099.
2 miles long.

Blackdown (NT)
1 mile south-east of Haslemere.
602 acres.

Buchan Country Park
South-west of Crawley off the A264.

Burton Pond Reserve
2½ miles south of Petworth off the
A285.

Chailey Common Reserve
8 miles north of Lewes, at the junction of
the A275 and A272.

Darwell Reservoir Trail (SWA)
4½ miles north-west of Battle of the
A2100.

Ditchling Common Country Park (STNC
and ESCC)
6 miles north of Brighton, 2 miles south
of Ditchling off the B2116.

Dyke Railway Trail (ESCC)
Starting at Aldrington Station.
4 miles long.

Eartham Wood Reserve (FC)
6 miles north-east of Chichester, 1 mile
north of Eartham off the A285.

East Head Trail (NT)
West Wittering, east side of Chichester
Harbour.
76 acres.

Ebernoe Common Reserve (STNC)
3 miles north of Petworth.
177 acres.

Fairmile Bottom Nature Trail (WSCC)
2 miles north of Slindon on the A29.
$1\frac{1}{2}$ miles long.

Footland Wood (FC)
8 miles north of Hastings on the S21, off
the B2089.
1 mile long.

Forest Way Nature Trail (ESCC)
From East Grinstead to Groombridge.
$9\frac{1}{2}$ miles long.

Friston Forest (FC)
Near Seven Sisters Country Park.
Leaflet available.
$2\frac{3}{4}$ miles long.

Goodwood Nature Trail
4 miles north of Chichester between
A286 and A285.

Gravetye Nature Trail (FC)
3 miles south-west of East Grinstead off
the B2110.
$1\frac{1}{2}$ miles long.

Hastings Country Park (Hastings
Borough Council)
Various trails, from Hastings to Pett.
228 acres.

Iping Common Reserve
2 miles west of Midhurst off the A272.

Kingley Vale Reserve (NCC)
3 miles north-west of Chichester at
Weststoke village.

Marden-Stoughton Down Trail (FC)
1 mile north-east of Stoughton, 8 miles
north-west of Chichester off the B2141.
$1\frac{1}{2}$ miles long.

The Mens Nature Reserve (STNC)
3 miles east of Petworth off the A272.
383 acres.

Napwood Nature Reserve (NT and
STNC)
4 miles south of Tunbridge Wells off the
A267.
107 acres.

Pagham Harbour Nature Reserve
(WSCC)
$4\frac{1}{2}$ miles south of Chichester off the
B2145.

Petworth Park (NT)
$5\frac{1}{2}$ miles east of Midhurst, at junction of
A272 and A283.
738 acres.

Rogate-Tullecombe (FC)
5 miles west of Midhurst off the A272.
$\frac{1}{2}$ mile long.

Rye Harbour Nature Reserve (STNC)
Between Winchelsea Beach and Rye
Harbour.
244 acres.

St Leonards Forest Reserve (STNC)
2 miles east of Horsham off the A264.
$13\frac{1}{2}$ acres.

Seaford Head Country Park (Lewes
District Council)
$1\frac{1}{2}$ miles south-east of Seaford off the
A259.
275 acres.

Selwyns Wood Reserve (STNC)
$1\frac{1}{2}$ miles south-west of Cross-In-Hand
off the B2102.
28 acres.

Seven Sisters Country Park (ESCC)
3 miles east of Seaford off the A259.
692 acres.

Shoreham Gap Nature Reserve (NT)
2 miles north-east of Shoreham.
596 acres.

Sidlesham Nature Trail
3 miles south of Chichester, $\frac{1}{2}$ mile
south of Sidlesham off the B2145.

Slindon-Selhurst Park (FC)
7 miles north-east of Chichester off the
A285 at Benges Corner.
2 miles.

Slinfold Trail
3½ miles north of Billingshurst off the
A29.

Tilgate Park
½ mile south of Crawley off the M23.
400 acres.

Tullcombe-Rogate Trail (FC)
5 miles west of Midhurst, off A272.
1½ miles long.

West Dean Trail (FC)
2 miles east of Seaford on A259, north at
Exceat Farm. Leaflet available.
2¾ miles long.

Woods Mill (STNC)
1½ miles south of Henfield on the
A2037.
15 acres.

Worth Way Trial
From Three Bridges to East Grinstead
on old railway track.
6 miles long.

PICNIC SITES AND VIEWPOINTS

Beachy Head
4½ miles south-west of Eastbourne.

Blackdown
8 miles north-east of Midhurst.

Butchersole Picnic Site
3 miles west of Eastbourne, off the
A259.

Chanctonbury Ring
½ mile south of A283, 3 miles west of
Steyning.

Devils Dyke
5 miles north-west of Brighton.

Ditchling Beacon
6 miles north of Brighton, 2 miles south
of Ditchling off the B2116.

Eartham Wood, Slindon
6 miles north-east of Chichester, 1 mile
north of Eartham off the A285.

Fairmile Bottom
2 miles north of Slindon on A29.

Finchfield, West Hoathly
5½ miles south of East Grinstead off the
A275.

Footlands Wood
8 miles north of Hastings off the B2980.

Friston Forest
Near Seven Sisters Country Park.

Gravetye Picnic Place
3 miles south-west of East Grinstead off
the B2110.

Halnaker
Picnic site at windmill, off the A285.

Harting Hill
1 mile south-east of South Harting on
B2141.

Hastings Country Park
From Hastings to Pett. Several sites.

Tullcombe Picnic Place, Rogate
5 miles west of Midhurst off the A272.

Seaford Head
From Seaford to Cuckmere Haven.

Selhurst Park, Slindon
7 miles north-east of Chichester at
Benges Corner.

Stoughton Down
8 miles north-west of Chichester, 1 mile
north-east of Stoughton.

The Trundle
1½ miles south of Singleton off the
A286.

West Dean
2 miles east of Seaford off the A259 near
Exceat Farm.

LOCAL EVENTS

January
Brighton: English Open Table Tennis
Championships
Hastings: International Chess Congress

February
Fontwell and Plumpton: National Hunt
Racing
Goodwood: Antique Dealers Fair

March

Brighton: Historic Motor Cycle Rally; Model Railway Exhibition; Southern Garden Show
Crawley: British Marbles Championships, Tinsley Green
Hastings: Competitive Music Festival

April

Bognor Regis: Drama Festival
Brighton: British Coach Rally; Brighton Races

May

Battle: Arts Festival
Brighton: Arts Festival; Historic Commercial Vehicle Rally; Brighton Races; Boat Show; MG Cars Rally
Eastbourne: International Folk Festival
Hastings: Rogationtide Ceremony 'Blessing of the Sea'
Hickstead: Showjumping

June

Ardingly: South of England Show
Arundel: Corpus Christi Carpet of Flowers
Bexhill and Hastings: Regattas
Brighton: Brighton Motor Rally; Brighton Races
Eastbourne: Womens International Tennis Tournament
Glyndebourne: Opera Season
Worthing: Bowls Championships
Goodwood: Inchcape International Dressage Championship; Antique Dealers Fair

July

Bexhill and Bognor Regis: Carnivals
Brighton: Antiques Fair; Stanmer Country Fair; Brighton Races; Lions Carnival
Charleston Manor: Arts Festival
Chichester: Southern Cathedrals Festival; Chichester Festival
Eastbourne: Carnival; County Tennis Championships
Goodwood: Horse Racing 'Goodwood Week'
Hastings: Carnival; Beer Festival
Hickstead: European Showjumping Championships
Littlehampton: Carnival

August

Alfriston: Cider Festival, Drusillas
Arundel: Festival; Arun Bath Tub Race
Brighton: Brighton Races; Antiques Fair
Bognor Regis: International Birdman Rally; Festival
Eastbourne: Eastbourne Show; Regatta; Cricket Week
Hastings: National Town Criers' Championships; Town and Country Fair; Festival; Old Town Carnival
Michelham Priory: Craft Fair
Rottingdean: Fair
Selsey: Crabbers Race
Worthing: National Bowls Championships

September

Alfriston: Festival of English Wine, Drusillas
Brighton: National Speed Trials
Findon: Sheep Fair
Petworth: Festival
Rye: Arts Festival

October

Brighton: International Tennis; Brighton Races
Chiddingly: Festival
Eastbourne: Autumn Flower Show
Hastings: Sussex Open Table Tennis Championships; Hastings Day Celebrations

November

Battle, Lewes and Rye: Bonfire Celebrations
Brighton: RAC Veteran car run from London
Eastbourne: Antiques Fair

December

Fontwell and Plumpton: National Hunt Racing

147

CYCLE HIRE

Bexhill: Cycleland, Tel: 217539
Bognor: Sandys Sport Centre, Tel: 823567
Brighton: Brighton Bike Hire, Tel: 728856
Chichester: Dugdales, Tel: 776751
Eastbourne: Rent-A-Bike, Tel: 34549
East Grinstead: Beddard Bicycles, Tel: 24409
Hastings: Cycle Hire, Tel: 434056, Rent-A-Cycle, Tel: 420006
Worthing: Rent-A-Ped, Tel: 208412

BOATING AND SAILING

There are clubs at the following centres:
Bexhill
Bosham
Brighton
Bognor
Chichester
Eastbourne
Felpham
Hastings
Lancing
Lewes
Littlehampton
Newhaven
Pagham
Pevensey Bay
Rye Harbour
Worthing

FISHING

Anglers may fish at all these places. However, permits must be obtained (see 'Useful Addresses'). Where permits are available on site this is indicated by *.

Abbots Lake, Arlington
Ardingly College and Reservoir*
Arlington Reservoir*
Balcombe Lake, Haywards Heath
Barcombe Mills
Barratts Park Farm, Heathfield*
Bennet Park Farm, Heathfield*
Bewl Bridge, Lamberhurst*
Boringwheel Fishery, Nutley*
Buckshole Reservoir, Hastings
Burton Mill Pond, Petworth
Chichester Canal
Clive Vale Reservoir, Hastings
Darwell Lake, Battle
Ecclesbourne Reservoir, Hastings
Farthings Lake, Battle
Fen Place Mill Estate, Nr East Grinstead
Furnace Brook, Cowbeech, Nr Hailsham*
Michelham Priory, Hailsham*
Newells Lake, Lower Beeding
Pevensey Haven
Piltdown Pond, Nr Uckfield. No Permit required
Piddinghoe Pond, Nr Lewes
Quarry Lake, Chichester
Scarlets Lake, Nr East Grinstead*
Shermanbury Place, Henfield
Southern Leisure Centre, Chichester*
Vale Bridge Mill Pond, Burgess Hill
Wallers Haven, Pevensey
Wattlehurst Lake, Nr Horsham
Weir Wood Reservoir, East Grinstead*
Whylands Farm, Battle*
Wishing Tree Reservoir, Hastings
Yew Tree Trout Fishery, Rotherfield*
River Arun
River Adur
River Cuckmere
River Ouse
River Rother (Eastern and Western)

Sea fishing is available all along the coast and boats may be hired at all the resorts.

TRANSPORT

East Kent Road Car Co, North Lane, Canterbury.
Tel: (0227) 66151

Green Line and London County, Lesbourne Road, Reigate, Surrey.
Tel: (07372) 42411

Hastings and District, Beaufort Road, Silverhill, Hastings.
Tel: (0424) 433711

Maidstone and District, Luton Road, Chatham, Kent.
Tel: (0634) 47334

National Express, 175 Rushey Green, Catford, London SE6.
Tel: (01) 730 0202

Southdown, Freshfield Road, Brighton.
Tel: (0273) 606711/606600

British Rail Enquiries
  West Malling, Tel: (0732) 842842
  Hastings, Tel: (0424) 429325
  Brighton, Tel: (0273) 25476
  London, Tel: (01) 928 5100

British Airports Authority, Gatwick Airport
Tel: (0293) 28822/31299

Sealink Services, Newhaven
Tel: (0273) 3166/4131

Automobile Assocition
Tel: (0273) 695231

Royal Automobile Club
Tel: (0273) 509253

Tourist Information Centres

Arundel, 61 High Street
Tel: (0903) 882268

Battle, 88 High Street
Tel: (04246) 3721

Bexhill-On-Sea, De La Warr Pavilion
Tel: (0424) 212023

Bognor Regis, 1/2 Place St Maur des Fosses, Belmont Street
Tel: (0243) 823140

Brighton, Marlborough House, 54 Old Steine
Tel: (0273) 23755 (weekends: 26450)

Chichester, St Peters Market, West Street
Tel: (0243) 775888

Eastbourne, 3 Cornfield Terrace
Tel: (0323) 27474

Hailsham, Area Library, Western Road
Tel: (0323) 840604

Hastings, 4 Robertson Terrace
Tel: (0424) 424242

Hove, Town Hall, Norton Road
(0273) 775400

Lewes, Lewes House, High Street
Tel: (07916) 71600

Littlehampton, Windmill Complex, The Green
Tel: (09064) 3480

Newhaven, Harbour Ferry Terminal Car Park
Tel: (07912) 7450

Peacehaven, Meridian Centre, Roderick Avenue
Tel: (07914) 2668

Pevensey Castle Car Park
Tel: (0323) 761444

Rye, Cinque Ports Street
Tel: (0797) 222293

Seaford, The Downs, Sutton Road
Tel: (0323) 892224

Shoreham, 86 High Street
Tel: (07917) 2086

Worthing, Town Hall, Chapel Road
Tel: (0903) 39999, ext 132/3

Worthing, Marine Parade
Tel: (0903) 39999 ext 372, or 210022

Youth Hostels

Alfriston, Frog Firle
Tel: (0323) 870423

Arundel, Warningcamp
Tel: (0903) 882204

Beachy Head, East Dean Road, Eastbourne
Tel: (0323) 20284

Guestling (Hastings), White Hart Hill
Tel: (042486) 2373

Patcham (Brighton), Patcham Place
Tel: (0273) 556196

Telscombe (Lewes), Bank Cottages
Tel: (0273) 37077

Truleigh Hill (Shoreham), Tottington
Barn
Tel: (0903) 813419

USEFUL ADDRESSES

English Heritage,
25 Savile Row,
London, W1X 2BT
Tel: 01 734 6010

Caravan Club,
East Grinstead House,
London Road,
East Grinstead
Tel: (0342) 26944

Countryside Commission,
John Dower House,
Crescent Place,
Cheltenham
Tel: (0242) 21381

Dinghy Cruising Association,
5 Ullswater Close,
Lightwater,
Surrey.

National Federation of Anglers,
Halliday House,
2 Wilson Street,
Derby
Tel: (0332) 362000

National Federation of Sea Anglers,
26 Downsview Crescent,
Uckfield,
Sussex
Tel: (0825) 3589

National Gardens Scheme,
57 Lower Belgrave Street,
London SW1W 0LR
Tel: 01 730 0359

National Trust, Regional Office,
Scotney Castle,
Lamberhurst,
Kent
Tel: (0892) 890651

Ramblers Assocation,
1-5 Wandsworth Road,
London SW8 2LJ
Tel: 01 582 6878

South East Arts,
9-10 Crescent Road,
Tunbridge Wells,
Kent
Tel: (0892) 41666

South East England Tourist Board,
1 Warwick Park,
Tunbridge Wells,
Kent
Tel: (0892) 40766

Southern Water Authority,
Guildbourne House,
Worthing,
Sussex
Tel: (0903) 205252

Sussex Archaeological Society,
Barbican House,
High Street,
Lewes
Tel: (07916) 4379

Sussex Industrial Archaeological Society,
Albion House,
Coburg Place,
Hastings
Tel: (0424) 436260

Sussex Ornithological Society,
Combe Cottage,
Mannings Heath,
Horsham
Tel: (0403) 3262

Sussex Trust for Nature Conservation,
Woods Mill,
Henfield,
West Sussex
Tel: (0273) 492630

YHA, Southern Region,
58 Streatham High Road,
London SW16 1DA
Tel: 01 769 0085

Bibliography

A History of Sussex, J. R. Armstrong (Darwen-Finlayson)

East Sussex, Iris Bryson-White (Spur Books)

Windmills of Kent and Sussex, Jim Cleland (Kindaim)

View of Sussex, Ben Darby (Robert Hale)

The Sussex Coast, Ian C. Hannah (Unwin)

Industrial Archaeology of South East England, A. J. Haselfoot (Batsford)

The Cinque Ports, Edward Hinings (Spur Books)

Highways and Byways in Sussex, E. V. Lucas (Macmillan)

The Cuckmere, Edna and Mac McCarthy (Lindel)

Standing Windmills of East Sussex, R. and R. McDermott (Betford Publications)

Standing Windmills of West Sussex, R. and R. McDermott (Betford Publications)

Monumental Brasses, Herbert Macklin (Allen and Unwin)

Sussex, S. P. B. Mais (Richards Press)

East Sussex, W. S. Mitchell (Shell Guides)

West Sussex, John Montgomery (Spur Books)

Sussex, Nairn and Pevsner (Penguin)

The Place-Names of Sussex, R. G. Roberts (Cambridge University Press)

The Folklore of Sussex, Jacqueline Simpson (Batsford)

Hidden Sussex, Swinfen and Arscott (BBC Radio Sussex Books)

Downs and Weald, J. F. P. Thornhill (Christophers)

A New History of Rye, L. A. Vidler (Goulden)

West Sussex Village Book, Tony Wales (Countryside Books)

The South East, John Talbot White (Eyre Methuen)

Sussex, Barbara Willard (Batsford)

Index

Abbots Wood, 144
Alfred The Great, 11, 90, 100
Alfriston, 51, 130
Amberley, 103
Anne of Cleves House, 63, 64, 137
'Antient Townes', 36
Apuldram, 114, 143
Ardingly, 83
Argos Hill Windmill, 78, 86, 141
Arlington, 55, 143, 144
Arundel, 95, 130, 134, 139
Ashburnham, 27
Ashdown Forest, 80, 86, 144

Barbican Museum, 63, 64, 137
Barlow Collection, 135
Barnsgate Manor Vineyard, 86, 142
Barrie, J.M., 80
Batemans, 28, 130
Battle, 29-33, 130, 135
Bayeaux Tapestry, 11, 18, 32, 43, 115
Bayham Abbey, 77
Beachy Head, 58, 144
Beckley, 35
Beeches Farm, 66, 133
Bell, Vanessa, 52
Belloc, Hilaire, 67, 71, 122
Benson, E.F., 38
Bentley Wildfowl Park, 54, 65, 139
Bepton, 188
Bewl Bridge Reservoir, 76, 144
Bexhill, 25, 135
Bignor, 102, 142
Billinghurst, 126, 146
Bishopstone, 52, 65
Black Down, 123, 144
Blake, William, 101
Blue Idol, 93, 130
Bluebell Railway, 83, 139, 140
Bodiam Castle, 30, 33, 130
Bognor Regis, 101
Bonfire Celebrations, 15, 64
Booth Museum, 70, 135
Borde Hill, 83, 86, 133
Bosham, 114, 143

Boxgrove, 101
Bracklesham, 114
Bramber, 88
Breaky Bottom Vineyard, 142
Brede, 42
Brickwall, 34, 42, 133
Bridge Cottage, 130
Brightling, 27
Brighton, 67-70, 135, 143
Brown, Capability, 82, 125, 134
Browne, Sir Anthony, 31, 32, 33, 78, 122
Buckleys Shop Museum, 60, 137
Bulverhythe, 25
Burgess Hill, 67
Burton Watermill, 125, 141
Burwash, 27, 140
Bury, 103
Butterfly Centre, 56, 58
Buxted, 66

Cade Street, 49
Camber Castle, 39, 42
Canute, 36, 115
Carr-Taylor Vineyard, 26, 142
Cat House, 71
Catsfield, 25
Chailey, 140, 144
Chalk Pits Museum, 103, 134
Chanctonbury, 91
Charles II, 68, 88, 94, 103, 117, 119
Charleston Manor and Farm, 52
Chelwood Gate, 87
Cherries Folk Museum, 42, 137
Chichester, 105-11, 135, 145
Chilsdown Vineyard, 142
Church Norton, 114
Cinque Ports, 11, 12, 18
Cissbury, 91, 142
Clayton, 67, 140
Climping, 101
Cobblers Garden, 86, 133
Cocking, 118
Cogidubnus, 105, 111
Conan Doyle, Sir Arthur, 80
Coolham, 93

Coombes Farm, 143
Coultershaw Waterwheel, 125
Cowdray, 122
Crawley, 129, 146
Cross-In-Hand Windmill, 49, 140, 145
Crowborough, 80
Crowhurst, 26
Cuckfield, 83

Dallington Sugar Loaf, 27
Danny, 65, 67, 130
De La Warr Pavilion, 25
De Montfort, Simon, 12, 62, 82
Dean Swift, 42
Debussy, Claud, 58
Denmans, 102, 133
Devils Dyke, 70, 72
Didling, 119
Ditchling, 65, 67, 144
Dolphinarium and Aquarium, 68, 139
Downers Vineyard, 143

Earnley Windmill, 114
Easebourne, 123
East Grinstead, 85
Eastbourne, 55-8
Ebernoe Horn Fair, 125, 145
Elgar, Sir Edward, 104
Engineerium, British, 71, 135
Etchingham, 28

Fairlight, 24
Fécamp, Abbey of, 18, 36
Felpham, 101
Findon, 93
Firle Place, 54, 65, 131
Fishbourne Roman Palace, 111, 142
Fishermans Museum, 20, 22
Fittleworth, 104
Fletcher, John, 37
Fletching, 82
Ford, 101
Forest Row, 87, 139
Forest Way, 86, 145
Fort Newhaven, 65, 143
Fox, George, 91
Frant, 78
Friston Forest, 51, 145
Fuller, 'Mad Jack', 27

Galsworthy, John, 103
Gibbon, Edward, 82

Gibbons, Grinling, 124
Gibraltar Tower, 48
Glyndbourne, 54
Glynde Place, 54, 65, 131
Goodwood, 116, 131, 145
Grange Museum, 72
Great Dixter, 34, 42, 131, 133
Greenwich Meridian, 72
Grimaldi, 23
Guestling, 41
Gunn, Martha, 68
Gunpowder, 32

Hailsham, 49, 136
Halland, 54
Halnaker Windmill, 102, 141
Hardham, 102, 104
Haremere Hall, 28, 131
Harold, 11, 31, 32, 115
Harrow Hill, 91
Hartfield, 82
Hastings, 18-24, 131, 136, 143, 144, 145
Hastings, Battle of, 1066, 32-4
Hawkhurst Gang, 37
Haywards Heath, 84, 85
Heaselands, 84
Heathfield, 48
Hellingly, 48
Henfield, 71, 136, 141
Herstmonceux, 46, 131, 133
Hickstead, 67
Highdown Chalk Garden, 91, 93, 133
Hollygate Cactus Nursery, 93, 133
Holtye, 86
Hooe, 46
Horam, 49
Horsham, 127, 136
Horsted Keynes, 83
Horsted Place, 66, 133
Houghton, 104
House of Pipes, 72, 90, 135
Hove, 71, 137, 144
Hurstpierpoint, 65

Icklesham, 41

Jack & Jill Windmills, 67, 72, 140
James, Henry, 38
Jekyll, Gertrude, 34, 84, 134

Kent & East Sussex Railway, 140
Keymer Windmill, 141

Kidbrooke Park Gardens, 86, 87, 133
Kingley Vale, 142, 145
Kings Mill, 141
Kipling, Rudyard, 28, 71
Kirdford, 125
Knepp Castle, 92
Knucker Hole, 101

Lamb House, 131
Lancing, 94
Laughton, 54
Legh Manor, 134
Leonardslee Gardens, 129, 134
Lewes, 61-4, 131, 137
Lewes, Battle of, 62
Lindfield, 85
Littlehampton, 100, 137
Living World, The, 52, 140
Long Man Chalk Figure, 50
Lordington House, 119
Lurgashall, 123
Lutyens, Sir Edwin, 34, 84
Lyminster, 101

Macmillan, Sir Harold, 87
Manor Costume Museum, 26
'Mapp & Lucia', 38
Marlipins, 91, 94, 138
Martello Towers, 46, 116
Mayfield, 78
Mermaid, The, 38
'Merry Andrew', 45-6
Merrydown, 49, 143
Michelham Priory, 49, 131, 134, 140
Midhurst, 120, 137, 145, 146
Milne, A.A., 82
Monks House, 64, 65, 131
Morris, William, 85
Mount Caburn, 61

Newhaven, 52, 65, 143
Newick Park, 66, 134
Newtimber Place, 132
Ninfield, 26
Normans Bay, 43
Northiam, 34
Nortons Farm, 138
Nutley Windmill, 83, 86, 141
Nymans Garden, 83, 134

Oasthouses, 14, 36, 42
Oates, Titus, 22

Old Clergy House, 51, 130
Old Mint House, 45, 132
Oldland Windmill, 72

Pagham, 114, 145
Paine, Tom, 63
Parham, 92, 134
Peacehaven, 72
Peasemarsh, 36
Penhurst, 27
Penn, William, 54, 91, 93
Perigoe Museum, 137
Pestalozzi Village, 33
Pett, 24
Petworth, 124, 132, 145
Pevensey, 43, 132
Piddinghoe, 64
Piltdown, 66
Playden, 36, 137
Polegate Windmill, 60, 137, 141
Potters Museum of Curiosity, 99, 135
Preston Manor, 71, 132
Priest House, 85, 132
Prince Regent, The 68
Pulborough, 104
Punnetts Town Windmill, 49

Racton Tower, 119
Rainbows End, 101, 139
Raystede Animal Sanctuary, 140
Repton, Humphrey, 78, 82, 87
Ringmer, 54
Robertsbridge, 28, 137
Rock Lodge Vineyard, 143
Rodmell, 64
Rossetti, Dante Gabriel, 24
Rotherfield, 79
Rottingdean, 71, 137, 141
Royal Observatory, 47
Royal Pavilion, 68, 132
Russell, Dr Richard, 67
Rye, 36-9, 137, 144
Rye Harbour, 40, 42, 145

Sackville College, 85, 86, 132
St Dunstan, 78
St Georges Vineyard, 30, 143
St Leonards Forest, 129, 145
St Leonards Mill, 41
St Mary's Hospital, 132
Salvington Windmill, 91, 93, 142
Seaford, 52, 145

Sedlescombe, 26, 33, 138
Selsey, 113, 141
Seven Sisters Country Park, 52, 60, 145
Sharpthorne, 85
Sheffield Park, 82, 86, 132, 134, 139, 140
Sheridan, Clare, 42
Shipley, 91
Shoreham, 94, 145
Sidlesham, 114, 145
Singleton, 117
Slot Machine Museum, 135
Sompting, 72, 94
South Harting, 119
Southease, 64
Spring Hill Wildfowl Park, 86, 87, 139
Standen, 85, 86, 132
Stanmer, 135
Steyning, 90
Stone Cross Windmill, 141
Stoolball, 54
Stopham, 104
Storrington, 92
Stoughton, 145
Sussex CCC, 71
Sussex Folklore Museum, 94, 138
Sussex Shirehorses, The, 144
Sussex Trug Baskets, 48
Sussex Trust for Nature Conservation, 71,
  72, 103, 146

Tangmere Military Aviation Museum, 138
Tarring, 91
Tanyard, 85
Telscombe, 72
Tennyson, 123
Ticehurst, 74
Toat Tower, 104
Trollope, Anthony, 119
Trotton, 120
Truleigh Hill, 91
Trundle, The, 105, 117

Turner, 124

Uckfield, 65, 130
Udimore, 41
University of Sussex, 135
Uppark, 119, 132

Valley Wine Cellars, 54, 143
Vespasian, 115
Veteran Car Run, 70
Volks Railway, 68, 70

Wadhurst, 74
Wakehurst Place, 83, 134
Warbleton, 19, 49
Warnham War Museum, 128, 138
Wartling, 46
Weald & Downland Museum, 117, 138
Webb, Philip, 85
Weir Wood Reservoir, 83
Wells, H.G., 119
West Blatchington Windmill, 71, 72, 141
West Dean Gardens, 134, 146
West Hoathly, 85
West Wittering, 114
Westfield, 42
Wilberforce, William, 88
Wilde, Oscar, 93
William the Conqueror, 30, 31, 32, 43, 115
Wilmington, 50, 138
Winchelsea, 40-1, 138
Windmill Hill, 48
Woods Mill, 71, 72, 146
Woolf, Virginia, 52, 64
Worth, 85, 146
Worthing, 93, 138
Wych Cross, 82, 87

Yapton, 101
Ypres Castle Museum, 36, 37, 38, 137

THE VISITOR'S GUIDE SERIES

- ☐ The Black Forest
- ☐ Brittany
- ☐ Chilterns
- ☐ Cornwall and Isles of Scilly
- ☐ Cotswolds
- ☐ Devon
- ☐ Dordogne
- ☐ East Anglia
- ☐ The French Coast
- ☐ Guernsey Alderney and Sark
- ☐ Hampshire & The Isle of Wight
- ☐ Historic Places of Wales
- ☐ Iceland
- ☐ Kent
- ☐ Lake District
- ☐ Loire
- ☐ North Wales and Snowdonia
- ☐ North York Moors, York & Yorkshire Coast
- ☐ Peak District (revised edition)
- ☐ Scottish Borders & Edinburgh
- ☐ Somerset & Dorset
- ☐ South & West Wales
- ☐ South of France
- ☐ Sussex
- ☐ Tyrol
- ☐ Welsh Borders
- ☐ Yorkshire Dales, Teesdale & Weardale

Touring Guide to Europe

A guide and travelling companion describing suggested itineraries through twenty-one countries in Europe, written for the discerning tourist on a low budget who prefers to seek out the less frequented places. It enables you to make the most from your holiday, whether journeying by car, train, bicycle or on foot.

The book sets out carefully selected itineraries through twenty-one countries, chosen for their scenic and cultural interest, together with detail on where to go and what to see.

- notes on the history, culture and customs of each country.
- information on touring, motoring, public transport, proposed routes for walking, cycling, mountaineering, skiing, etc.
- recommended places to visit in the major cities, with plans.
- emphasis on touring routes specially chosen for their scenic and cultural interest to enable you to plan a holiday and make the most from your visit.
- advice on food and drink.

Countries covered: Austria, Belgium, Denmark, England and Wales, Finland, France, Germany, Greece, Iceland, Irish Republic, Northern Ireland, Italy, Luxembourg, Netherlands, Norway, Portugal, Scotland, Spain, Sweden, Switzerland, Yugoslavia.

- ★ **approx 480 pages, plus 61 maps**
- ★ **specially chosen touring routes**
- ★ **general information for motorists, ramblers, cyclists, skiers**

Moorland Publishing, Station Street, Ashbourne, Derbyshire. Tel: (0335 44486).